The Economic Function of a Stock Exchange

Zicklin School of Business Financial Markets Series

Robert A. Schwartz, Editor
Zicklin School of Business
Baruch College/CUNY
New York, NY, USA

For other titles published in this series, go to
www.springer.com/series/7133

Robert A. Schwartz • John Aidan Byrne
Lauren Wheatley
Editors

The Economic Function of a Stock Exchange

Springer

Editors
Robert A. Schwartz
Zicklin School of Business
Baruch College/CUNY
New York, NY
USA

John Aidan Byrne
New York, NY
USA

Lauren Wheatley
Zicklin School of Business
Baruch College/CUNY
New York, NY
USA

ISBN 978-3-319-10349-5 e-ISBN 978-3-319-10350-1
DOI 10.1007/978-3-319-10350-1
Springer Cham Heidelberg New York Dordrecht London

Library of Congress Control Number: 2014954251

Printed on acid-free paper

Springer is part of Springer Science+Business Media (www.springer.com)

Price Discovery: The Economic Function of a Stock Exchange[1]

We all know a stock exchange when we see it. The challenge is offering a clear and concise definition of a stock exchange. According to Webster's Dictionary, a stock exchange is a place where security trading is conducted on an organized system. Armed with this information (and not having a clue what Webster was telling us!), we googled "organized system." We came upon a couple of entries dealing with health and the like, at the top was "book binding." So that's it—a stock exchange is a place where we bind the books. It sure beats cooking them!

A further search with Google produced a sizable amount of description on a stock exchange, specifically with this insight: an exchange is an association of stock brokers who meet and transact business according to recognized forms and regulations. We can certainly do better than this was our immediate thought.

A better approach to defining an exchange, we concluded, was to focus on the economic service that the institution provides. And that brings us to the title of this paper: What is the economic function of a stock exchange? Being Baruch professors, we offer the following multiple choice question:

The economic function of a stock exchange is to:

1. Handle transactions with reasonable speed at reasonable cost (this one obviously has to be correct).
2. Find the two sides of a trade (well, quantity discovery does matter).
3. Produce the price (price discovery certainly is important).

[1] This chapter is a slightly amended paper of the same title by Nasli Sila Alan and Robert A. Schwartz, published in the *Journal of Portfolio Management,* Fall 2013. The paper was developed from Schwartz's Opening Comments at this 2011 Baruch conference in New York City. Reprinted with permission from the *Journal of Portfolio Management.*

4. Facilitate capital raising in the primary market (it is uncontestable that a vibrant IPO market is vitally critical for a country's economic growth).
5. All of the above (this one drives our students crazy).

The answer? Number 5, of course, "All of the above."

Of course, this is not the kind of pithy definition we were searching for. After a bit more head scratching, we decided to drill down on just one of the answers—Number 3, "Produce the price." And bingo, we had our definition: an exchange is the venue where share prices for listed securities are discovered. In this paper, we delve into some of the economic thinking that underlies this definition.

PRICE DISCOVERY IS A PUBLIC GOOD

We start by considering the economic importance of an exchange produced price. Given the multiple uses to which a discovered price is put, efficient price discovery is critically important, not just to those who participate in a trade but to a far more extensive set of people. An exchange produced price is used for:

- Marking-to-market
- Derivative pricing
- Valuations of mutual fund cash flow
- Estate valuations
- Dark pool pricing

Because the beneficiaries include a wide range of people who are not participating in the transactions that establish a price, an economist would refer to an exchange produced price as a *public good*. A classic example of a public good is the lighthouse in a harbor. Any ship passing in the night can see the lighthouse. Who among us would suggest that the light in the lighthouse be selectively shut off? You simply do not tell a ship's captain, "No, you are not allowed to see the light because you did not pay to see it." The lighthouse is standing there on a rock, and all passing ships are consumers of the service that it provides but does not directly charge for. The lighthouse is a public good.

We like the lighthouse image because an exchange-discovered price shines light on the value of shares for the broad public.[2] The idea is the same—a broad spectrum of market participants looking at an exchange

[2] For earlier mention of the lighthouse image in the context of price discovery, see Robert A. Schwartz, "Dark Pools and Fragmented Markets," World Federation of Exchanges, 2009 Annual Report and Statistics.

produced price, and a ship's captain spotting a lighthouse, all gain valuable information without directly paying for it.[3] It is extremely important to remember this. So why hasn't price discovery received more attention given its critical role as a public good? Of course, there is some analysis in the academic literature and a bit of hand waving on the topic as well, and the term "price discovery" does come up at times in regulatory discussions and documents. Nevertheless, the concept of an exchange-produced price being a public good receives woefully inadequate attention in public debates about market structure.

THE COMPLEXITY OF PRICE DISCOVERY

How difficult is price discovery, one might enquire? For a simple reason, price discovery is complicated and should not be taken for granted. We all talk about fundamental values, and about prices at times decoupling from fundamental values, but stocks do not have fundamental values. How can we say this? We will answer this question with a question: Do people agree in their stock analyses? Consider this: About 2:00 pm on April 4, 2013, Apple shares traded at $429.38. Did all investors at that time believe that Apple shares were worth $429.38 exactly? Before we answer let us first explain. Clearly, if we all agree about the inputs of a model, we will all get the same answers and thereby reach the same conclusions. But do we agree about the inputs? Do we all even use the same models? What happens if we do not?

The academic term that characterizes total agreement is "homogeneous expectations." If investors do not have homogeneous expectations, the term used is "divergent expectations." So, which is it, homogeneous expectations or divergent expectations? We think the latter (note that any disagreement about this would only serve to support our point). Of course, homogeneous expectations is a useful assumption for much modeling (e.g., the Capital Asset Pricing Model). Moreover, some academicians believe that the assumption is not unrealistic (identically informed and rational players, the argument goes, should all reach the same conclusions). But evidence is widespread that expectations are divergent. We hear substantial debate and disagreement among investors, commentators, and stock analysts about share values. We attribute this to the enormous size, complexity, inexactitude, and incompleteness of the information set. Accordingly, the divergent

[3] Stock price data are, of course, sold by exchanges and bought by customers who want instant delivery, along with academicians who use trade and quote data for academic research.

expectations environment is the one that we wish to operate within and better understand (see Davis et al. (2007) for further discussion).

Now, if people disagree about a stock's share value, wherein lies its *fundamental* value? Answer: nowhere. In a divergent expectations world, the market is there to find, not fundamental values, but equilibrium prices. That is, prices which harmonize the desires of a continuum of disparate bulls and bears to hold shares. Finding these prices is what a stock exchange does, and fulfilling this function is not a simple matter.

MARKET STRUCTURE MATTERS

Recognizing that the quality of price discovery is important, one might still question whether or not quality depends on the architecture of a marketplace. The answer is clear: the efficiency with which prices are discovered very much depends on the procedures, rules, and regulations that govern how orders are submitted, brought together, and turned into trades. For instance, the priority rules of order execution (price, time, size, etc.), the temporal consolidation of orders in call auction trading, the use of stock specific trading halts and across the board circuit breakers, all determine how orders interact. In so doing, all these establish trades and transaction prices. Three recent enactments by the Securities and Exchange Commission, along with remarkable technological developments, have intensified inter-market competition. These enactments were the Order Handling Rules of 1997; Regulation Alternative Trading Systems of 1998, and Regulation NMS (which includes the trade-through rule) fully implemented by 2007. This combination of regulations and technology has fragmented the marketplace, primarily for NYSE issues. The order flow is integrated differently in a fragmented marketplace and, thus, price discovery can be affected. In a later section, we consider the effect that NASDAQ's opening and closing calls (instituted in 2004) have had on price volatility at market openings and closings.

Market structure change, whether caused by technology developments, regulation, and/or competitive pressures, can be assessed in terms of market characteristics such as trading costs (e.g., commissions, spreads, and market impact costs), consolidation/fragmentation of the order flow, pre- and post-trade transparency, market robustness/fragility, fairness, and the quality of price discovery. The quality of price discovery relates to each of its predecessors on the list: trading at disequilibrium prices is a trading cost; noisy price discovery obfuscates market transparency; price discovery is more apt to spin out of control in a fragile marketplace; and poorly discovered prices are fair neither to traders who are active in the market nor to the broad market that uses exchange prices for a spectrum of non-trading purposes (As we have noted, an exchange produced price is a public good).

We suggest that good quality price discovery be placed high on the regulatory priority list. With a sharper focus on price discovery, the other market characteristics should more readily fall into place. However, being high on the list comes with a necessary precondition that the objective be operational, which leads to a very key question: How can we assess the quality of price discovery? What can be used as a benchmark?

INFERRING THE QUALITY OF PRICE DISCOVERY

Only God knows what the equilibrium price may be, mere mortals cannot see it. Unfortunately, because we are not able to quantify the deviations of actual prices from unobservable equilibrium values, there is a tendency not to study market quality in terms of the efficiency of price discovery. Unobservability is indeed a debilitating reality from both an academic and a regulatory perspective. But all is not lost! We can assess the accuracy of price discovery by focusing on very short-period, intraday price volatility.

The efficiency of price discovery can be *inferred* from the level of intraday price volatility. That's because intraday volatility is accentuated by microstructure factors, most notably bid-ask spreads, market impact, and price discovery noise. Critically, the accentuation is too large to be explained entirely by spreads and market impact, especially in the neighborhood of market openings and closings. The dominant factor, in our opinion, is price discovery noise, particularly at market openings. This is at a time when, following the advent of overnight news, finding "the price" is most challenged on a daily basis.

It is well established that intraday volatility follows a U-shaped pattern. In fact, the U-shape is so severe that, in the opening and closing minutes, volatility shoots up sharply and the intraday pattern is more stapled-shaped than U-shaped. As noted, we attribute the opening spike to the complexity of price discovery (while the closing spike is largely a consequence of traders trying to "get the job done" before the market closes).

We stress the importance of analyzing intraday volatility and its implications for price discovery when a market is under stress. For it is at a time such as this that the complexities of price discovery are brought to light. In relatively calm periods, price discovery is not as big an issue, and the quality of a trading system is not particularly challenged. We hone in on stress by focusing on the first half hour of trading and, in the section after the next that follows, by showing the price record for a stock (Disney) that, on a specific day (August 10, 2011), exhibited extraordinarily high first half-hour volatility.

A SPECIFIC STOCK/DAY VIEW OF OPENING VOLATILITY

The opening volatility spike, in and of itself, indicates the complexity of price discovery. In Exhibit 1, we present some stock/day specific examples of opening half-hour volatility for a sample of the Dow 30 stocks. To select these stocks, we first calculated the opening volatility measure and a spread-adjusted volatility measure for all US stocks for each trading day in 2011:

$$\textit{Opening Volatility} = \frac{P^{\max} - P^{\min}}{P^{mean}} \tag{1}$$

$$\textit{Adjusted Volatility} = \frac{P^{\max} - P^{\min} - \textit{Spread}}{P^{mean}} \tag{2}$$

For a given stock on a given day, P^{max}, P^{min}, and P^{mean} denote, respectively, the highest, the lowest, and the average trade prices during the opening half hour of trading (from 9:30AM to 10:00AM). *Spread* is the time-weighted average bid-ask spread during the opening interval for a specific stock and a specific day. Our opening high-low volatility measure captures the range of price movements over this intense 30-min period of the trading day. We adjust the measure by subtracting the spread from the interval's high–low in order to obtain a volatility measure that is net of the bid-ask spread.

After getting volatility values for each of the stocks on each of the days, we sort the stocks by their adjusted volatility and divide the observations into 20 equally sized groups. Group 1 contains the stock/day observations with the lowest adjusted volatility, and Group 20 contains the observations with the highest adjusted volatility. We next impose a price filter that restricts the sample of stocks to the \$30 to \$100 price range and select only the Dow stocks. From these stocks, we present data for the highest observation in each of the 20 groups (no Dow stock falls into the four groups with the lowest volatility). In so doing, we allow each specific Dow stock and each specific calendar date to be represented in the exhibit only once.[4] This selection process results in 16 observations, which are shown in Exhibit 1, with the observations arrayed from the least volatile to the most volatile.

[4] In order to have our selected examples represent different stocks and days, we employ the following: Once a stock/day is selected as the top observation for a group (starting from Group 20 through Group 1), all remaining observations for that stock and day are excluded from the sample that is used for selecting the top observation of the next group.

Company name (Ticker)	Date	Avg price	Hi-Lo	Spread	Volatility (%)	Adjusted volatility (%)	Group[a]
Johnson & Johnson (JNJ)	04/06/11	$59.82	$0.20	$0.01	0.33	0.31	5
Boeing (BA)	06/29/11	$72.34	$0.38	$0.03	0.53	0.49	6
Home Depot (HD)	04/20/11	$38.34	$0.25	$0.01	0.65	0.62	7
Merck (MRK)	09/27/11	$32.06	$0.25	$0.01	0.78	0.74	8
Travelers Companies (TRV)	08/04/11	$53.32	$0.48	$0.02	0.90	0.86	9
Exxon Mobil (XOM)	05/26/11	$81.92	$0.82	$0.01	1.00	0.99	10
Procter & Gamble (PG)	04/12/11	$62.52	$0.71	$0.01	1.14	1.12	11
McDonalds (MCD)	10/05/11	$86.19	$1.12	$0.04	1.30	1.26	12
Walmart (WMT)	01/20/11	$55.66	$0.80	$0.01	1.44	1.41	13
American Express (AXP)	09/26/11	$46.59	$0.77	$0.03	1.65	1.60	14
United Technologies (UTX)	02/24/11	$82.74	$1.53	$0.03	1.85	1.81	15
United Health Group (UNH)	12/08/11	$49.25	$1.05	$0.02	2.13	2.08	16
Verizon (VZ)	08/01/11	$35.80	$0.89	$0.01	2.49	2.46	17
Du Pont (DD)	08/05/11	$47.88	$1.45	$0.02	3.03	2.99	18
Jpmorgan Chase (JPM)	08/25/11	$37.69	$1.57	$0.01	4.17	4.14	19
Disney (DIS)	08/10/11	$30.34	$2.31	$0.02	7.61	7.55 %	20

Exhibit 1 Selected stock/day examples of opening volatility
[a]There are no Dow stock observations in the first four groups; therefore, our table starts from Group 5.

Exhibit 1 gives the company name and ticker, date of the observation, average price during the opening half hour, the dollar difference between the highest and the lowest price, the time-weighted average spread, opening volatility, spread-adjusted opening volatility, and the group to which the observation belongs. For example, on April 6, 2011, Johnson & Johnson (a $60 stock) was in the lowest volatility group, with a $0.20 price fluctuation in the first half hour, a spread of $0.01 (2 basis points), and an adjusted volatility of 0.31 %. At the other end of the spectrum, Disney (a $30 stock), on August 10th, experienced a $2.31 price fluctuation in the first half hour of trading with a spread of only 2 cents (7 basis points). Concurrently, its adjusted high–low was a substantial 7.55 %! For all 16 observations, the non-spread related price movements displayed in Exhibit 1 are indicative of a component of volatility that represents appreciable price discovery noise. In the next section, we consider the Disney experience in greater detail to gain further insight, for a market under stress, as to whether the large price fluctuations are attributable largely to news or to dynamic price discovery.

THE DISNEY (DIS) EXPERIENCE

The four highest adjusted volatility entries in Exhibit 1 are for August 2011, a time when the markets were profoundly rattled by the European debt crisis. Might this explain the high first half-hour volatility? Macro uncertainty is certainly an underlying causal factor, precisely because price discovery is more difficult at times when uncertainty is high and people have diverging expectations about what the future will bring. Nevertheless, the question remains: What could account for one person buying shares at a price that was 7.61 % percent higher than the price at which someone else sold shares within the same half hour when the average spread was only $.02, as occurred on August 10 for Disney stock? Was a fresh news release from Europe or any other news event during that particular half hour the cause? A search of LexisNexis revealed no major news announcements at this time for either Disney or the broad market.

Neither does Disney's price path suggest the advent of a major news announcement in the opening 30 min of trading on August 10. Exhibit 2 shows, second-by-second, for that first half hour, how Disney's (DIS) price evolved, side-by-side with the price of the SPDR S&P 500 ETF (SPY). To suppress the effect of price changes attributable to the bid-ask spread and to reduce the effect of out of sequence reporting, the prices shown in the exhibit are averages for all trades that occurred in each of the 1,800 s that comprise the first half hour. (On that day, DIS averaged 37 trades per second, while SPY averaged 124 trades per second). In Exhibit 2, DIS's prices are on the left hand axis and its chart is the solid line; SPY's prices are on the right hand axis and its chart is the dashed line.

For DIS, there is initial volatility and a bump up in the first minute, a predominantly downtrend until 9:37AM, a predominantly uptrend until 9:50AM, falling prices for the next couple of minutes, and lastly an uptrend to 10:00AM. The picture for SPY is simpler: falling prices until 9:35AM, an upward trend until 9:48AM, and falling prices to 10:00AM. Comprehensively viewed, both paths display mixtures of trending and reversals, and the two paths appear to be weakly correlated. In fact, the returns implied by these price movements are correlated: for 30 s returns, the correlation is .19, and for one minute returns the correlation is .47.

We thus infer that intra-half-hour news release is not the cause of the observed price movements for DIS; rather, the cause is dynamic price discovery. Apparently, the August 10 opening price did not adequately reflect the broad market's desire to hold Disney shares. The substantial price changes which ensued for at least the next 30 min largely reflected the market searching for a price that better balanced the opposing pressures of a diverse population of buyers and sellers.

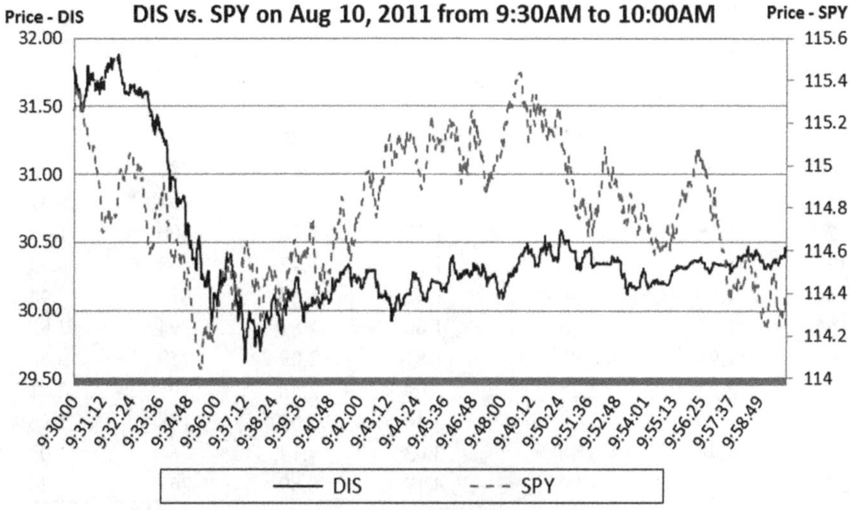

Exhibit 2 Price path for SPY vs. DIS during the opening half-hour interval on August 10, 2011

THE DOW 30 EXPERIENCE

Having focused on one stock (DIS) in particular, we now consider the full set of 30 Dow stocks over all 252 trading days in 2011. In this assessment, each stock/day observation is assigned to a volatility group, and the same stock can fall into different volatility groups on different days. The summary statistics of the adjusted opening volatility for each of these groups are given in Exhibit 3. Except for the three highest volatility groups, the means and medians are virtually identical. Referring to the mean, adjusted volatility ranges from 0.28 % for the lowest volatility group to 5.56 % for the highest volatility group. The faster rise in volatility among the higher volatility groups is striking: while Group 18 has an average volatility of 2.71 %, the average reaches 3.49 % in Group 19 and 5.56 % in Group 20. Exhibit 3 also shows the number (N) and the percent (%N) of Dow observations in each of the 20 groups. Out of the volatility observations for all Dow stocks in 2011, about 43 % fall into groups 11 through 20; in 2011. In other words, almost half of the Dow stocks experienced an opening volatility that is higher than the median volatility across all stocks. Clearly, it is not just the small-cap stocks that experience high volatility, the largest stocks of the economy are also affected by price discovery noise.

Group[a]	Mean (%)	Median (%)	Min (%)	Max (%)	N[b] (%)	% N
5	0.28	0.28	0.16	0.31	77	1.02
6	0.42	0.42	0.32	0.49	607	8.03
7	0.56	0.56	0.49	0.62	939	12.42
8	0.68	0.68	0.62	0.74	1,032	13.65
9	0.80	0.80	0.75	0.86	854	11.30
10	0.92	0.92	0.87	0.99	780	10.32
11	1.05	1.05	0.99	1.12	754	9.97
12	1.18	1.18	1.12	1.26	600	7.94
13	1.33	1.33	1.26	1.42	503	6.65
14	1.50	1.49	1.42	1.60	412	5.45
15	1.70	1.70	1.60	1.81	294	3.89
16	1.94	1.93	1.81	2.09	259	3.43
17	2.25	2.24	2.09	2.46	197	2.61
18	2.71	2.68	2.46	3.02	148	1.96
19	3.49	3.40	3.03	4.14	78	1.03
20	5.56	4.86	4.19	8.89	26	0.34

Exhibit 3 Summary statistics of the adjusted opening volatility by group

[a]There are no Dow stock observations in the first four groups; therefore, our table starts from Group 5

[b]Total number of observations is 7,560 (30 stocks * 252 trading days)

NASDAQ'S CONTROLLED EXPERIMENT

Further insight into price discovery noise can be gained by assessing the effect a new trading procedure has on the intraday volatility metric. If a new procedure lowers intraday volatility, one can infer that intraday volatility had been unduly accentuated in the first place (with price discovery noise being the major causal factor). NASDAQ presented a good controlled experiment for this analysis when, in 2004, it introduced its opening and closing crosses.[5]

Pagano, Peng, and Schwartz (2013) have examined the effect of NASDAQ's calls on opening and closing price volatility. Comparing a

[5] Although NASDAQ refers to these new facilities as "crosses," they are indeed price discovery calls and we will refer to them as such.

pre-call period (February 2004) to a post-call period (February 2005), they find that 1-min volatility has decreased for both the opening and the closing minutes of the trading day. They write:

> "Taking the large-cap stocks as an example, for the last five one-minute intervals before the close, the declines in the median range are 3.1, 4.2, 4.8, 1.7, and 12.6 basis points, respectively, all are statistically significant, and they correspond to 23 %, 30 %, 32 %, 12 %, and 34 % decreases relative to their levels in February 2004. For the opening intervals, the pattern of volatility reduction is stronger for the large-cap stocks and somewhat weaker for the mid- and small-cap stocks. For the large-cap stocks and for the first three one-minute intervals at the market's open, the reductions in the median range are 6.0, 9.1, and 3.8 basis points (using transaction price data), respectively, and they are all statistically significant at the .01 level. This translates into 11 %, 22 %, and 13 % decreases relative to their corresponding levels in February 2004."[6]

NASDAQ's introduction of opening and closing calls is a major market structure innovation, positively and significantly affecting price discovery. Indeed, the superiority of a trading system is recognizably manifest in reduced intraday volatility, supporting the importance of dampening this metric by sharpening price discovery. Once again, we stress that accurate price discovery should be a top priority goal for market architects and regulators. With this thought, we next consider how intraday volatility has evolved in recent years.

THE EVOLUTION OF VOLATILITY OVER TIME

Intraday volatility can be further assessed by tracking its changes over time, an approach that we have followed in Alan and Schwartz (2013).[7] Exhibit 4 presents these findings for the evolution of opening half-hour price volatility for NYSE and NASDAQ stocks over the period 1993–2011. Once again, the volatility measure used for this analysis is the opening volatility (percentage high–low price range given in Eq. (1)) and a VIX-adjusted opening volatility metric (percentage high–low price range divided by the VIX to control for underlying market volatility). Panel A of Exhibit 4 presents the monthly average opening volatility for NYSE and NASDAQ stocks over

[6] The median range mentioned in the quote refers to the opening volatility measure used in this paper and defined as the percentage high–low price range over an interval (similar to our opening volatility).

[7] Focusing primarily on the opening half hour of the trading day, Alan and Schwartz have constructed five volatility measures in total for three separate periodicities (i.e., daily, monthly, and over two subsections of the sample period). The various measures tell a fairly consistent story.

the last two decades, and Panel B presents the same comparison for VIX-adjusted opening volatility. Both graphs show that volatility is not declining for NYSE stocks—it is rising. This finding is compatible with Story and Bowley (2011) who, in calling attention to the recent high level of market volatility, note how the *New York Times* reported, "price fluctuations of 4 % or more during intraday sessions have occurred nearly six times more than they did on average in the four decades leading up to 2000."

NASDAQ stocks show evidence of a different pattern. In 1993, NASDAQ's volatility was well above that of the NYSE. Since then, it swings around quite a bit and, after about April 2004, it shows a slight downward trend. Notice how the two lines in Exhibit 4 have come together in recent years. Currently, the NASDAQ and NYSE markets are looking very similar in this regard although this was not so in 1993. This outcome is striking; it suggests that price discovery efficiency has deteriorated at the NYSE but not at NASDAQ. Perhaps the key factor that distinguishes the NASDAQ experience from that of the NYSE is that NASDAQ's marketplace has historically been relatively fragmented, while the Big Board's market share for its stocks declined from over 80 % in 1993 to under 30 % in 2011 [as discussed in Alan and Schwartz (2013)].

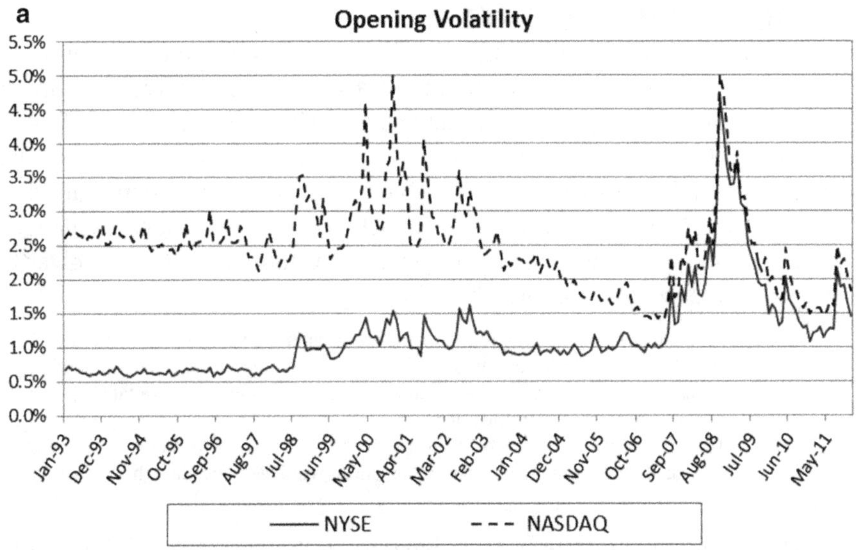

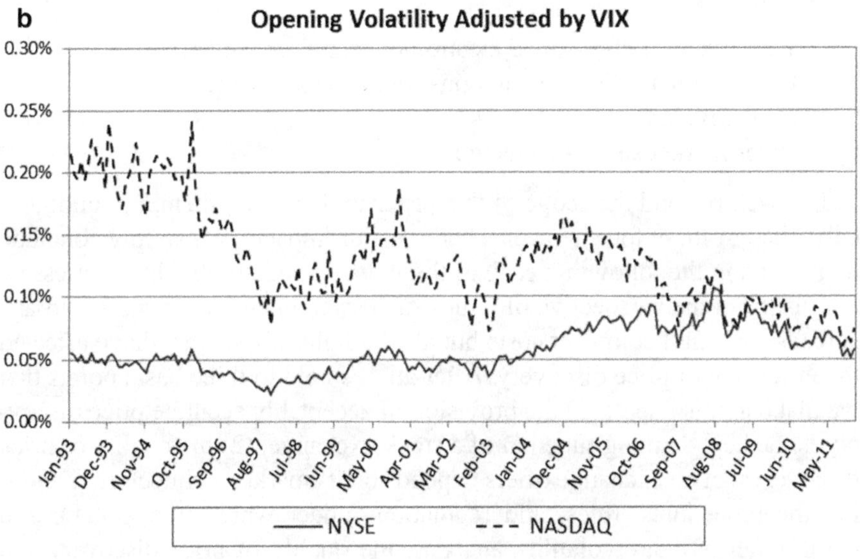

Exhibit 4 ***Panel A*****: Average opening volatility of NYSE vs. NASDAQ stocks.** ***Panel B*****: Average VIX-adjusted opening volatility of NYSE vs. NASDAQ stocks**

A FOUR WORD ANSWER

About a quarter of a century ago, William Freund, then chief economist at the New York Stock Exchange, organized a seminar on market structure at the NYSE for a small group of academicians. (There weren't many of us in the field at the time). William (Mil) Batten, the NYSE's Chairman, joined the seminar for a full day of discussions. One of the questions Freund raised at that gathering: What is the economic service provided by a stock exchange? The title of this paper was inspired by that question. One of us (Schwartz) who was at that seminar reports the following:

> Mil didn't speak much at that event but he was a good listener. I had my thoughts because I was already involved in price discovery, but wanted to hear if anyone else would mention it. So I was listening, and Mil was listening, and the other academicians were talking, and nobody was saying anything about price discovery.
>
> Then Mil raised his hand and uttered, 'We produce the price.' Yes, Mil! Eureka, I thought to myself. Ever since, his four-word answer has stuck with me. The thought is terribly important.

We have one final question: How have the following affected the quality of price discovery?

1. The advent of high-speed electronic technology and HFT
2. Increased market fragmentation—both spatial and temporal
3. New government regulations
4. Other market structure changes

It is well beyond the scope of this paper to delve into them, but undoubtedly, each of these four items has had a major impact.[8] We simply conclude by reiterating the following: each of these developments should be assessed, not just from the perspective of issues such as competition, fairness, bid-ask spreads, and market impact costs but also in light of how they have affected the efficiency of price discovery. After all, we hold to three basic points that we make in this paper: (1) the provision of acceptably accurate price discovery is the key, defining function of a stock exchange; (2) the quality of price discovery that an exchange offers depends on its market architecture (including the procedures, rules, and regulations under which it operates); and (3) through intraday volatility analysis, the quality of price discovery can be assessed.

Robert Schwartz

[8] For a recent discussion of high-frequency trading, see Schwartz and Wu (2013).

References

Alan NS, Schwartz RA (2013) The evolving quality of the equity markets: an intraday volatility analysis. Working paper, Baruch College

Davis P, Pagano MS, Schwartz RA (2007) Divergent expectations. J Portfolio Manag 34(1):84–95 (Reprinted in Journal of Trading, Vol. 3, No. 1, (Winter 2008), pp. 56–66)

Pagano MS, Peng L, Schwartz RA (2013) A call auction's impact on price formation and order routing: evidence from the NASDAQ Stock Market. J Financ Market 16(2): 331–361

Schwartz RA (2009) Dark pools and fragmented markets. World Federation of Exchanges, Annual Report and Statistics

Schwartz RA, Wu L (2013) Equity trading in the fast lane: the staccato alternative. J Portfolio Manag, forthcoming

Story L, Bowley G (2011) Market swings are becoming new standard. New York Times, September 12, 201.

List of Participants

Name	Organization	Title
Alfred Berkeley	Pipeline Trading Systems *At the time of the conference, Alfred Berkeley was with Pipeline Trading Systems	Chairman & CEO
William Brodsky	Chicago Board Options Exchange	Chairman & CEO
Andrew Brooks	T. Rowe Price Associates, Inc.	Vice President and Head of Equity Trading
Joe Cangemi	ConvergEx Group	Managing Director, Head of Global Electronic Equity Trading and Sales
Ian Domowitz	ITG	Managing Director, Analytical Products and Research
Pinar Emirdag	London Stock Exchange Group	Head of Professional Business Development
Huseyin Erkan	Istanbul Stock Exchange	Chairman & CEO
Reto Francioni	Deutsch Börse AG	CEO
Joseph Hall	Davis Polk & Wardwell LLP	Partner
Bill Harts	Thomson Reuters *At the time of the conference, Bill Harts was with Thomson Reuters	Chief Strategy Officer, Sales & Trading Division
Frank Hatheway	NASDAQ OMX	Chief Economist
Alasdair Haynes	Chi-X Europe *At the time of the conference, Alasdair Haynes was with Chi-X Europe	CEO
Rob Howe	Liquidnet	Corporate Strategy

(continued)

Name	Organization	Title
Peter Jenkins	AX Trading Network, LLC *At the time of the conference, Peter Jenkins was with AX Trading Network, LLC	President
Gary Katz	International Securities Exchange	CEO
Larry Leibowitz	NYSE Euronext *At the time of the conference, Larry Leibowitz was with NYSE Euronext	COO
Timothy J. Mahoney	BIDS Trading	CEO
William O'Brien	Direct Edge	CEO
Brett Redfearn	J.P. Morgan Securities	Global Head of Liquidity
Joe Rosen	RKA, Inc.	President
Asani Sarkar	Federal Reserve Bank of New York	Research Officer
Robert A. Schwartz	Zicklin School of Business, Baruch College, CUNY	Speiser Professor of Finance
Barry E. Silbert	SecondMarket Inc.	Founder & CEO
Gary Stone	Bloomberg Tradebook LLC	Chief Strategy Officer
John Wally Sullivan	Pulse Trading	Managing Partner
Larry Tabb	TABB Group	Founder & CEO
Bruce Weber	Lerner College of Business and Economics, Univeristy of Delaware	Dean
David Weild IV	IssuWorks, Inc.	Founder & Chairman
Gregory L. Wright	ThinkEquity LLC	CEO
Steve Wunsch	Wunsch Auction Systems	Principal Investor

Conference Sponsors

AX Trading Network
BIDS Trading
Bloomberg Tradebook LLC
Chicago Board of Options
Direct Edge
International Securities Exchange
ITG
Liquidnet
NASDAQ OMX
NYSE Euronext
Pipeline Trading Systems
TABB Group

Contents

CHAPTER 1: OPENING ADDRESS: FUTURES AND OPTIONS MARKETS IN THE EVOLUTION OF STOCK EXCHANGES

William Brodsky, *Chicago Board Options Exchange*

I do not know how many of you are familiar with the person Bernard Baruch, after whom this august institution is named. As a matter of fact, my father attended Baruch, so it is dear to my heart. Dad always talked in awe about Bernard Baruch. Not surprisingly, it is a pleasure to be here before you today.

As I was preparing my remarks, I decided that it was time for me to learn more about this famous historical financial figure, Bernard Baruch.[1] He was indeed a remarkable individual. He was originally a poor guy who came to New York, and who eventually made his way into our financial markets. Baruch worked in the stock and the commodities markets. I read about how he became a very successful investor. Some people called him a speculator, but actually, he believed in fundamental investing.

Today, some people would call Baruch a high-frequency trader. Do you know what he once did? He was on the Jersey Shore in 1898 when he learned about a stock that was expected to rise in value. The stock exchange was closed because it was a holiday. Imagine the scene. Here he is on the Jersey Shore back when telephones were not as ubiquitous as today. Baruch wanted to get to his office in New York so he could send a cable to London with the U.S. markets closed. So what did he do? He wanted to catch a train, but the trains weren't running because of the holiday schedule.

His solution? He literally commandeered a train, and hired some people to take him to New York on a train alone! I don't even know if that was legal. In any event, he made his way to New York and to his office on Wall Street from where he sent a cable to London and bought the stock ahead of everyone else. Insider trading? Absolutely not. He just had a hunch that the market was

[1] Recommended reading: Bernard M. Baruch. The Adventures of a Wall Street Legend. (John Wiley & Sons, Inc., 1997.)

R.A. Schwartz et al. (eds.), *The Economic Function of a Stock Exchange*, Zicklin School of Business Financial Markets Series, DOI 10.1007/978-3-319-10350-1_1

going to open higher the following morning. Baruch, in his early days, was able to figure out how to invest in a particular stock before other people.

I tell you this story because this controversy today about high-frequency trading, among other things, relates a lot to market structure today. But it is no different today than the carrier pigeons used during the early days of the Rothschilds.[2] There is always someone who will find a faster way to do a transaction. Anyone who thinks they will find ways to slow things down is really defying the natural proclivity of technology and of people seeking to be a little bit faster than someone else. To try to say that everyone is going to move in lockstep at the same moment in time is unrealistic.

Professor Schwartz, first of all, it is great to be here with you. When I was Chairman of the World Federation of Exchanges (WFE) in 2009–2010, we inaugurated a Life Time Achievement award.[3] The first recipient of that award was you for your work in market structure. You continue to do tremendous work. I applaud you for that. (Applause).

So when Bob asked me if I would come speak today, I said why are you asking me? I am from the Chicago Board Options Exchange, the CBOE. We are an options exchange. We do options and some futures products, but this conference is about stock exchanges. So, what am I supposed to talk about? Well, I did start my career on Wall Street in the stock brokerage business, and then I worked at the American Stock Exchange. So I said to Bob, if it works for you, I would like to talk about the role of futures and options markets in the evolution of stock exchanges. When I grew up in New York and Bill Freund was chief economist of the NYSE, there were stock exchanges and there were commodity exchanges. The two were very different. Over time, not only has that changed, but my thesis today is that the evolution of the futures and options markets has forever altered the role of the stock exchanges.

I will start with ancient history and then continue into modern times. Going back to the 1600's, there were stock exchanges in Amsterdam, London, Frankfurt, Paris and elsewhere. (I won't go through all of them). Then there were commodity exchanges that operated very separately from the stock exchanges. In Osaka, Japan, there was a rice futures exchange. It was the first futures exchange in the world, although they didn't call it a futures exchange.

[2] During the nineteenth century, at its height and earliest days, the Rothschild family is believed to have had the largest private fortune in the world.

[3] Trade association of 57 publicly regulated stock, futures and options exchanges as of writing. http://www.world-exchanges.org/about-wfe.

Many of the futures exchanges were product specific. In London, there was a coal exchange and a corn exchange. In Chicago, we had the Chicago Board of Trade (CBOT) for grains only. COMEX, the Commodity Exchange, only did metals. Remember COMEX? And the Chicago Mercantile Exchange (CME), at one time, was the butter and egg exchange, in other words a produce exchange.[4]

Then what happened? It wasn't until 1972 that the concept of commodities exchanges started morphing away from solely commodities into financial futures markets. The CME started the International Monetary Market (IMM) to trade currency futures. The Board of Trade, struggling with having basically only one product line (agricultural commodities), tried to figure out how they could trade futures on stocks. The Securities and Exchange Commission said, "No, no, no, you can't do that, you can't trade futures on stocks." Their response? They said, they would trade options on stocks. There was a small over-the-counter put and call market in New York in those days. There was not much price transparency. You had to look in the newspaper for advertisements on options prices. It took the CBOE 5 years to get through the SEC approval process.[5] Those of you who work with the SEC today will not be surprised to hear that.

Then, shortly afterwards, because the Chicago Mercantile Exchange had started down the path of financial futures, the Commodity Futures Trading Commission (CFTC) was formed in 1974. Think about it: The CBOE was created before there even was a CFTC. But because the CBOE's options were deemed securities by the SEC, some of the older U.S. stock markets looked at that as a possible avenue of growth. At that time, the American Stock Exchange (AMEX) was second to the New York Stock Exchange (NYSE), and it was very hard for the AMEX to grow their stock business. So they said, let's do this new thing called options.

Over the next few years, the American Stock Exchange, the Philadelphia, Pacific, and the Midwest Exchange (now the Chicago Stock Exchange), followed the CBOE and began trading options. In Europe, the first exchange outside the U.S. to trade standardized options was the Amsterdam-based

[4] CME Group, globally headquartered in Chicago, is today ranked as the world's leading derivatives marketplace offering a diverse range of futures and options products for risk management. CME is today part of the CME Group. http://www.cmegroup.com/company/history/.

[5] The CBOE was formed in 1973 becoming the first U, S. marketplace for trading listed options. http://www.cboe.com/.

European Options Exchange.[6] Amsterdam is particularly interesting because it is where the first organized options market had started in the 1600's. After the CBOE was started, there were exchanges created to trade either options on stocks or futures on financial products, but virtually never at a pre-existing stock exchange. For example, in London it was LIFFE, in Paris it was MATIF, in Spain it was MEFF, in Singapore it was Simex, in Switzerland it was SOFFEX.[7] Why weren't the stock exchanges creating these markets? One of the reasons was because the stock exchanges viewed themselves as being something apart, something different—and even better—than these secondary or tertiary markets that were called futures or options markets.

What were the characteristics that allowed financial products to be traded on exchanges? When I joined the CME, the products were not called "contracts," they were called "cars." I once asked, what's a car?[8] I was told that it's a railroad car. You see, you had a railroad carload. It was a car and they would ask how many cars are you trading? And I would respond, "What are you talking about?" They were trading S&P futures contracts and they would call them cars. It didn't make sense to me. The mentality was agricultural. But it was the agricultural structure of the futures markets that allowed for the creation of financial futures and options.

What were some of these characteristics? The most basic characteristic was standardized contract terms. For example, there was May wheat.

[6] In 1978, the Amsterdam Stock Exchange Association launched the European Options Exchange. This was the first options exchange in Europe and only the second worldwide. In 2000, The Amsterdam Exchange merged with the Brussels and Paris exchanges to create Euronext N.V., part of NYSE Euronext, and the first pan-European exchange.

[7] LIFFE, the London International Financial Futures and Options Exchange, a futures exchange based in London, is now part of NYSE Euronext. That follows its takeover by Euronext in January 2002 and Euronext's subsequent merger with New York Stock Exchange in April 2007.
MATIF, the Marche a Terme International de France, was a French futures exchange that became part of the Paris Bourse in 1999. A year later it merged with the Amsterdam and Brussels exchanges to form Euronext NV. Euronext merged with the NYSE Group in 2007 to form NYSE Euronext.
MEFF, the Mercado Español de Futuros Financieros, better known as MEFF, is an electronic trading exchange in Spain formed in 1989 and facilitating trading, clearing and settlement of futures and options in single stocks and equity indexes, including the benchmark Ibex 35.
Simex, the Singapore International Monetary Exchange, became part of the Singapore Exchange in 1999.
SOFFEX, the Swiss Options and Financial Futures Exchange, which later became part of Eurex, was launched in 1988 for the electronic trading of electronic derivatives and equities.

[8] The speaker joined CME in 1982 as executive vice president and COO.

Everyone understood May wheat—wheat that was delivered in May. How about the IBM March 160 call—that was standardized? There weren't 20 different brokers offering IBM options that expired on different days of a particular month. It was the same day in March. It was a 160 strike price, and it was a call option. And that was the essence of the standardization concept.

The second standardization term was next day settlement. That might not seem surprising today, but in those days, in 1972, stocks settled in five days, and in London it was fortnightly settlement. Think about that. What facilitated next day settlement was "certificateless" trading. Because you needed five days to settle stocks, you had little old men running around with pieces of paper delivering stock certificates in 1972 and 1973! And then, most importantly, the additional part, which today they call the "plumbing," is that there was a dedicated clearing house.

The clearing house in the futures world was so very important because it intermediated the risk between the buyer and the seller. Remember, in stock transactions, there is a buyer and a seller, and there is virtually no risk. Once the stock is paid for, you take the shares, put them in your vault, and forget about them. But with an option or future, it is an expiring product, and you needed to value it on a regular basis. And so, in the options and futures worlds, a clearing house stood between the buyer and the seller, and you didn't have to worry about whether the obligation would be fulfilled. Additionally, there was what was called the daily mark to market by the clearing house.

It is remarkable how far-sighted that was back then—if you think about what happened between Lehman and AIG with no one knowing what the value of a contract was.[9] There was no independent third party to make an evaluation. In this recent crisis, it was the firms making their own determinations of what these things were worth. In fact, at central clearing houses, in some cases, on highly volatile days it is not just the daily mark to market; there are also intraday margin calls.

Once again, the stock markets didn't pay a lot of attention until the mid- to late-1970's. That is when the New York Stock Exchange said, you know these guys out in Chicago are trading T-Bonds, T-Bills, and futures. They are trading Ginnie Mae futures. And options on IBM, General Electric and Coca-Cola– and those are our stocks! Seeing this, the New York Stock Exchange decided to create a futures exchange called the New York Futures

[9] See, A Weapon of Mass Destruction Strikes: Credit Default Swaps Bring Down AIG and Lehman Brothers. Jerome A Madden. *Business Law Brief.* Fall 2008. http://www.wcl.american.edu/blr/documents/Fall08_AWeaponofMassDestructionStrikes.pdf.

Exchange.[10] But the NYSE didn't have a cadre of market-makers the way that the Chicago exchanges did because the specialist system, by definition, was a solitary franchise.

What existed in the Chicago markets were many market makers with no one market having a priority over the other. It was easy to get a new product started because people could go from one product to another. You didn't need a franchise to trade an IBM option, or a Ginnie Mae future. This was Chicago style trading—open outcry pit trading without a central specialist as market maker.

I was at the AMEX at the time the exchanges decided that, if they wanted to get into the options business, they couldn't do it without a single specialist. So they actually tried to sell seats. They did sell seats, but they weren't really successful because the New York community didn't understand what these new seats were intended to do. They understood specialists, but they didn't understand competing market makers.

The other thing that was a deterrent to stock exchanges getting into the options and futures business, besides their general inclination that we trade the real thing—stocks—was this: stock exchanges evolved historically where companies came to them and said, please here is my company, I'd like to list our stock. The stock exchange replied: well let me see if you meet our criteria. And, by the way, we charge for this service. You have to pay us to list your shares. In the futures and options markets, the exchange had to design a contract, so they started hiring economists, not to analyze markets, but to create new products. That was a very different thing than what was common in stock exchanges back in those days.

There also were vast cultural differences. For example, the SEC had already existed for many years back in the 1970's, while the CFTC was brand new. There were different regulatory regimes in the U.S. and other foreign markets. In the U.S., the SEC and CFTC had very different philosophical approaches to regulation. In Japan, it was the Ministry of Finance versus the Ministry of Trade and Industry. The same thing existed in Australia and in Taiwan. Different regulatory structures for these different markets existed even though the underlyings' instruments were equity products or government bonds. In other countries—Germany, is my best example—trading futures contracts was illegal. There were other markets in the world that wanted to trade these new products, but that couldn't because there were rules (some of which were 200-years-old) that didn't allow it. And in the U.S., the concept of cash settlement was new. Australia was the first

[10] Formed in 1979.

county that allowed cash settlement as a way of having these traded products settled.

In the U.S., it took the Shad-Johnson Accord[11] to allow for cash settlement for stock index futures contracts. Without that legislative change, it couldn't have happened. And then we had dramatic changes in the governance of exchanges, which brings me to a much more recent period.

Exchanges, be they stock exchanges or futures or options markets, particularly in this country, operated as not-for-profit member organizations. They were run by the members and, very often, for the benefit of the members. There were changes to the securities laws by the federal government under the Securities Act Amendments of 1975.[12] The reality was that, as not-for-profit organizations, the value of the exchanges was in the memberships, not in the ability of the exchanges to operate as for-profit institutions. If you think back even 10 years ago before the exchanges demutualized, the value of a seat was the value to the members of having access—that is, trading rights—to an exchange, which is not uniquely tied to the enterprise value of the exchange.[13]

Now what about products? Where were the products created, and how did that evolve? Once again, my thesis is that most of the innovation in these financial derivatives markets took place in Chicago between 1972 and 1982. Foreign exchange, which had been tried a little bit in New York, became much more successful at the CME in their IMM (International Monetary Market) division. There were interest rates, first Ginnie Mae's and then T-Bonds, T-Bills, and, when cash settlement came about, there were Eurodollar futures based on LIBOR. Stock indexes followed, which actually started in Kansas City with the Value Line Index, and in New York with the NYSE Composite Index. The CME became the most successful futures exchange, probably because it had the best index, the S&P 500, which represented the benchmark of the U.S. stock market—and the deepest pool of traders.

For options, one of the aspects I found the most interesting when I studied the CBOE history, is that they knew that they wanted to trade options on

[11] The 1982 Shad-Johnson Accord established the CFTC's right to regulate futures contracts on major stock indexes, an achievement of historic proportions since it was the first time the SEC had ceded authority over an equity-based financial instrument.

[12] Enacted in June 1975 to amend the Securities Exchange Act of 1934. It directed the Securities and Exchange Commission, together with the industry, to create a National Market System as well as a nationwide system for the clearance and settlement of securities transactions.

[13] Demutualization is the process of moving from being a mutual company owned by its exchange members to a company owned by shareholders.

stocks because they weren't allowed to trade futures on stocks. But it took them a while to figure out exactly what it was they were going to trade. All of a sudden the light bulb went off, and they said we will trade the premium because they weren't exactly sure how to trade an option on the stock. You know it's a call, but what exactly are you trading? They finally came to understand that what you are really trading is the premium of the put or call option.

Another interesting development that occurred while the CBOE and the listed options markets were forming was the publication of the Black Scholes pricing model in 1973.[14] Remember, the Nobel Prize in Economics wasn't awarded until 1997, but Fisher Black and Myron Scholes came together with Robert Merton to develop an equation, or a theory on the pricing of options. The formula had no relation to the launch of the CBOE. It was intended to assist corporations in valuing options that they granted to their executives. But a dynamite confluence of events occurred that would impact the growth of the listed-options industry. These events were the creation of the CBOE, the publication in the financial journals of the Black Scholes Model, and the Texas Instruments hand held calculator that allowed for the rapid calculation of options. IBM stock, for example, will change price hundreds of times during a day. How did that affect the price of an IBM May 160 call? The call's price was also changing all the time. The Texas Instruments calculator allowed the early market makers to keep their valuations up to date. And then index options and index futures came about. These were very exciting changes, indeed.

Another noteworthy development: the CBOE was an instant success and the American Stock Exchange wanted to get into the business. The SEC did not want to have all these separate clearing houses because they had just gone through the back office paper work crunch of the late 1960's and early 1970's. So the Option Clearing Corporation (OCC), which was jointly owned by all of the options exchanges, was formed.[15] We then had this for the first time—fungibility. That is, an option contract bought on one exchange could be sold on another exchange. That was another development which is still pretty unique, particularly if you look at other countries. What were the ingredients that made these markets so successful? In thinking about this, remember that, throughout this period, these options and futures exchanges were still very separate from the stock exchanges.

Stock exchanges remained focused on listing the companies, and little by little, automating some of their trading systems. What was unique about these

[14] One of the most significant concepts in modern financial theory.

[15] Formed in 1973.

derivatives markets, particularly in the U.S, was that some of these things were then exported elsewhere in a spirit that I call, "the culture of risk taking." A lot of this happened both here in New York and in Chicago. There were traders on floors that didn't have any special franchise who learned how to hedge their positions. They would buy one option, and they'd sell another. They were hedging themselves off. For instance, they would buy a stock and sell a call, or engage a myriad of other strategies.

In the history and the development of the U.S. stock exchanges, the specialist was at the center, and you were either long or you were short; there was nothing in between. Even as the options markets developed, the specialist community in New York did not embrace it by saying, gosh, we have this big long position, how do we hedge it over the weekend? It seemed obvious to those of us who understood it, but it wasn't being practiced.

The next significant development to impact the industry was the creation of the trading firms, founded by some of the brightest people from the floors. Three firms specifically that came to mind as I was preparing for this conference: O'Connor & Associates, Chicago Research and Trading (CRT), and Hull Trading. O'Connor & Associates came right off of the CBOE floor. O'Connor was ultimately purchased by Swiss Bank Corp.; CRT wound up being acquired by Nations Bank and then Hull Trading by Goldman Sachs. Blair Hull of Hull Trading was one of the first to automate options market making. Right before the IPO that he was planning, he went and sold the company to Goldman.

Then there was internationalization. Within a few short years, there were 50 exchanges around the world that traded futures and options. Once again, in most cases, they were not associated with a stock exchange. The growth was tremendous, and it continued. What really changed over the last few years is that, as companies and exchanges started to go public, they realized that there was much more value in combining the cash and derivatives businesses. So, in certain countries, the stock exchanges and the futures and options exchanges came together.

I could go through the list, but Bob is giving me a warning that I have to move along a bit more quickly. I think that the most important change in the last ten years was demutualization which took the exchanges from their value being in the seats, to their value from being an exchange itself. Other important changes were automation and how exchanges went public. This changed the governance structures and made them much more competitive. Automation and demutualization have allowed for a lot of the dramatic changes that we have seen, and for the coming together of the options, futures and stock exchanges.

So, one of my thesis today is that, even though the stock exchanges previously resisted embracing options and futures, combining them made sense. And once demutualization and IPOs occurred, it became very evident that the options markets and the future markets were growing faster than the stock markets. And because they were also very profitable, the stock exchanges had to do something about it. I believe that the engine of growth for many traditional stock exchanges that are still considered stock exchanges is really coming from their derivatives markets.

I have a few slides that show where we are today and how futures and options changed the world of stock exchanges. This is from World Federation of Exchanges (WFE) data. If anyone wants to drill down more, look at the 2010 WFE data, it is about a 40-page slide deck. From these, I have taken three slides to show you [See, Exhibit 1 for all 3 Slides]. First, the global derivative markets had a 26% growth rate in 2010—with 11.3 billion futures and 11.1 billion options traded. Asia has surpassed Europe and the Americas in total volume. Stunning numbers! The data are laid out by product group (Exhibit 1).

Equity derivatives represent the largest category in terms of contracts traded, but they represent a small percentage of notional value. I think that what is important is that interest rates, by definition, have a large notional value. Volume is probably a more telling number. Let me just give you a couple of highlights of where the volumes are. The most active equity index options in the world are in Korea, at the National Stock Exchange of India, and at the CBOE. The most active index futures are at the CME, Eurex, Russia, and India. ETF options are totally dominated by the U.S. There is a bit of action in Canada, and a little bit in Brazil. However, ETF options are a very fast growing area. Interest rates are dominated by CME, LIFFE and Brazil, and FX by Russia, India, CME and Brazil. Turning to commodities, it is most significant that of the top five exchanges, three are Chinese. China will be a tremendous growth area in these derivatives markets.

The last thing under the category of WFE statistics is "exotics." I am happy to say that we are at the center of that. CBOE created a way to trade volatility. We've developed a formula to calculate equity market volatility, by using options traded on the S&P 500. From that number we now trade futures and options on volatility. The index is well known, it is the VIX.[16] CBOE dominates it; the second largest is Eurex.

[16] The well-known measure of the implied volatility of S&P 500 index options, VIX is the trademarked ticker symbol for the Chicago Board Options Exchange Market Volatility Index.

a

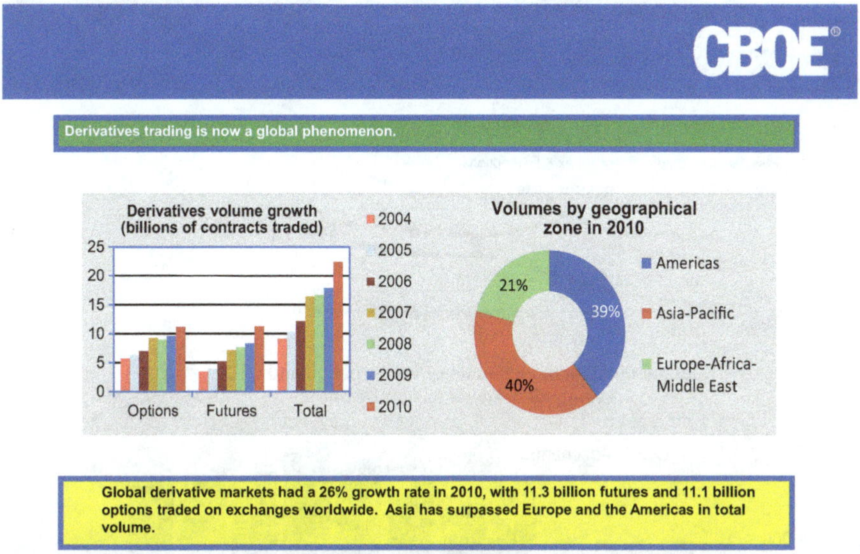

b

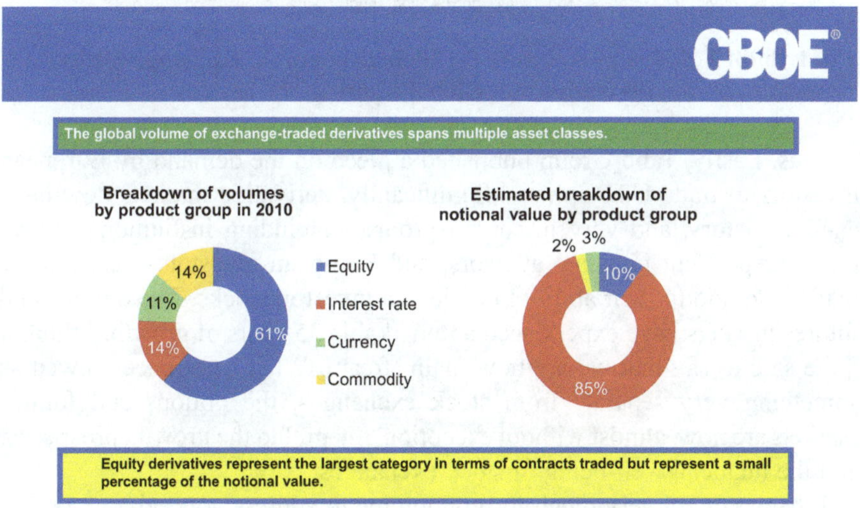

Exhibit 1 (continued)

The bottom line is that there is tremendous growth in these markets. There are studies on the growth potential of the options markets. One is on institutional investors by the Tower Group. Another is by Bellomy Research which noted that independent financial advisors are increasing their use of

c

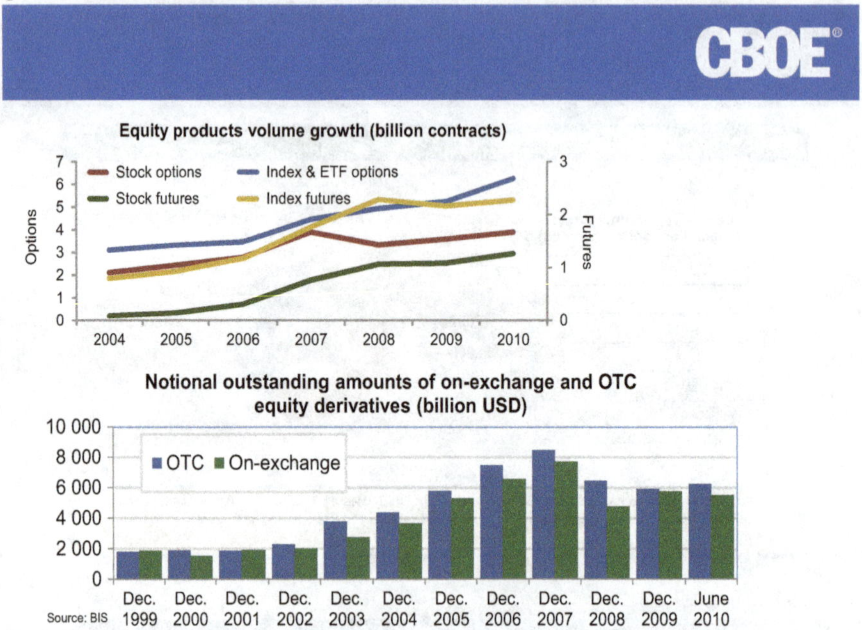

Exhibit 1 Industry structure (a) Globalization, (b) Exchange-traded derivatives, (c) Global equity derivatives

options. Lastly, Tabb Group published a piece on the demand by European investors to trade U.S. options. Significantly, derivative markets now have enough history, and very important groups—including institutional investors, independent financial advisors, and European investors—using these markets to add to their ability to trade and invest in stocks. The options and futures markets have experienced a remarkable 35 years of growth. I think it quite safe to say that we are now main stream. What were once viewed as something very separate from stock exchanges, the options and futures markets are now, almost without exception, integral to the growth, prosperity, and the financial well-being of stock exchanges.

I thank you all very much for inviting me to address you today.

CHAPTER 2: WHAT MAKES AN EXCHANGE A UNIQUE INSTITUTION?

Moderator: Andrew Brooks, *T. Rowe Price Associates, Inc*
Alfred Berkeley, *Pipeline Trading Systems, LLC*
Gary Katz, *International Securities Exchange*
William O'Brien, *Direct Edge*
Brett Redfearn, *J.P. Morgan Securities*
Asani Sarkar, *Federal Reserve Bank of New York*

ANDY BROOKS: An exchange throughout history has performed a number of unique functions in the trading of securities. These functions have included finding the opening and closing process; halts; dissemination of news; pending news; dealing with the order of balances, sources of information on supply and demand; aggregation of buyers and sellers; price discovery; transparency; speed; fair and orderly markets; reconciliation; and arbitration. These and much more might have been seen as unique in the past. However, I am not sure that is the case today. I want to start by asking each of our panelists this question: In your view, what makes an exchange unique? Let's start with Al.

ALFRED BERKELEY: It is all about the rules of engagement. Exchanges provide an environment. We have a lot of different exchanges, and they all provide different environments. They compete on that basis. That environment consists of a set of trading rules that professionals coming to an exchange and trading in the markets agree to follow. These become the rules of engagement. It is all about who knows what; when do they know it; and what can they do with this knowledge when they know something. Professor Bill Wilhelm of the University of Virginia wrote a wonderful book called *Information Markets*.[1] He points out three ways in which people cooperate

This chapter is a slightly amended paper of the same title by Robert A. Schwartz and John Aidan Byrne, published in the *Journal of Trading,* Winter 2014. The paper was developed from the panel presented in this chapter. Reprinted with permission from the *Journal of Trading*.

[1] Information Markets (Harvard Business School Press, 2001), William J. Wilhelm Jr., outlines how advances in information technology are transforming financial markets.

R.A. Schwartz et al. (eds.), *The Economic Function of a Stock Exchange*, Zicklin School of Business Financial Markets Series, DOI 10.1007/978-3-319-10350-1_2

on a satisfactory trade. One is coercion by the government, or an exchange. Thus, the government would say you must do this, or that, and it has the power to enforce its mandate. An exchange, by its rules, takes the same approach once you've agreed to be a participant. The rules coerce you to perform in a particular way under pain of being excluded. Second, and at the other end of the spectrum, is natural cooperation. That's when people are dealing repeatedly with each other and discipline each other through social norms and/or through economic interaction. Third is a middle ground. This is where most exchanges sit. The middle ground involves the intermediation of a human agent, a trusted agent who knows more than one participant, and more than both players in a trade. He knows more because he is constantly dealing with those same people. Actually, he develops a reputation for how he deals with people, and this can be a win-win.

You have these rules of engagement, the human interaction from dealing repeatedly with the same person. This is very difficult to achieve in an anonymous electronic environment where you don't know who you are dealing with over and over again. In that sense, the rules of the exchange have to change to compensate for the lack of personal knowledge.

GARY KATZ: What makes an exchange unique? To me it is similar to the concept of a brand. What makes us look at the logo of a very popular company and instantaneously recognize what that stands for? It is the brand of the company. Exchanges are, in essence, a brand. When we ask what is unique about exchanges, we're really asking what is the brand that you immediately recognize as the characteristic that an exchange represents.

What's unique about all exchanges worldwide are two very important features. One is that they are non-discriminatory. They treat all of their members the same. The second is transparency. That transparency follows from how members are treated. And it also refers to how the assets trading on that exchange are handled on a daily basis. It doesn't matter whether these are commodities; it doesn't matter if they are futures, options or equities. Transparency is the brand that defines an exchange.

WILLIAM O'BRIEN: I think of exchanges as one of the original social media institutions. We talk about the world becoming more social, right? There's Facebook, and a host of other types of social media. But exchanges were one of the original institutions of that nature. In modern times, in financial market regulation, you think about exchanges and compliance as being inextricably interwoven. Exchanges were originally voluntary institutions. Exchanges were user communities coming together under defined yet flexible rules that allowed the participants to move forward, commercially and/or professionally. It also moved forward the lives of the people who mattered to exchange participants, whether these people were customers of these participants or investors generally. That continues to this day. That is what really makes exchanges unique among the other companies that intermediate the financial markets.

BRETT REDFEARN: In my opinion, the basic function of any exchange (stock or otherwise) is to provide infrastructure, market data, or the price as Bob [Schwartz] would say, and a regulatory environment for the fair and orderly trading of securities. In some cases—and it varies in different locations—an exchange is there for clearing and settlement services.

Today, you also see the provision of technologies either to the members, or to the customers of the exchanges and, in many cases, to competitors as well. However, it is worth noting the evolution of exchanges over time. The answer to this question today would be different than the answer 50 years ago, or even 20 years ago, as exchanges have evolved. The changes include the technology, trading practices, and the regulations that have enabled significant competition for the exchanges from other venues including Electronic Communications Networks, ECNs and Alternative Trading Systems, ATSs.[2]

ASANI SARKAR: Bob Schwartz, I remember some years ago you had a conference on volatility. That was pretty much right after we had the crash that erupted in 2008![3]

(Laughter)

BROOKS: I am certainly glad we are not talking about volatility today!

SARKAR: And then this year we have the topic of exchanges at the same time as we have the Dodd-Frank Act [4] on the horizon. This act is

[2] Reg ATS, introduced by the SEC in 1998, aims to protect investors and regulate this type of trading system. The regulation has strict record keeping and reporting requirements on areas such as transparency once an ATS reaches more than 5% of the trading volume in any security. Examples of ATSs include Electronic Communication Networks (ECNs), crossing networks and call markets.

[3] The Dow Jones Industrial Average plunged 777.68 points, the most in one single day on September 29, 2008, as the financial crisis that started in 2007, and with its roots in subprime mortgages and toxic debt, sent shock waves through the markets. On October 23, 2008, Baruch College hosted a conference on **Volatility**, organized by **Robert A. Schwartz**, Speiser Professor of Finance at Baruch College's Zicklin School of Business.

[4] Dodd-Frank Wall Street Reform and Consumer Protection Act, known as Dodd-Frank, was signed into law by President Barack Obama on July 21, 2010. The sweeping consumer protection and regulatory reform law also includes the controversial Volcker Rule that prohibits proprietary trading by depository banks. The final regulations of the Volcker Rule were published in the Federal Register on January 31, 2014, to take affect on April 1, 2014. See, Volcker Rule, OCC Bulletin, 2014-9, March 25, 2014. http://www.occ.gov/news-issuances/bulletins/2014/bulletin-2014-9.html.

proposing to move a lot of these over-the-counter derivative securities to exchanges. Once again, the focus of the conference is highly appropriate. I look forward to your conference next year!

For the past year or so I have been working with colleagues at the New York Fed on some very detailed data on credit derivatives swaps, or CDSs.[5] As you know, these are OTC transactions. They are very different from how exchange-listed securities are traded. We have been looking at the data, trying to see whether these OTC transactions would benefit from the unique characteristics of the exchange.

One unique service the exchange provides is simplicity. Let me explain. A stock exchange provides a product that is highly standardized. For example, shares of IBM are identical to each other, and the terms of the "contract" are highly standardized. You don't have to worry whether one share of IBM means something different from any other share. All of these products are coded in exactly the same way. If the price of a share is $100 today and it's $101 tomorrow, you don't have to worry about whether the prices being quoted are different. In this regard, the OTC world is quite different from the stock exchange world. In many respects, the OTC contracts are not standardized. If you buy a share of a CDS from a dealer today, and then you buy a CDS on the same company from a different dealer on another day, there is no guarantee that those two contracts will have identical terms. Nor would they necessarily be quoted in the same way.

The other thing that allows for simplicity on an exchange is the design of the market structure. This goes back to what Al and Gary were saying about the rules of engagement. At an exchange, I don't have to worry about whom I am trading with, about who my counterparty is. The reason is that my counterparty is really the exchange. I can buy a share of Morgan Stanley today. If I change my mind, I can sell it tomorrow. I have zero economic exposure. I can go into and out of an economic exposure very rapidly without worrying about who my counterparty is. This is very different from an OTC world where transactions are bilateral.[6] You are always dealing with a specific intermediary.

Basically the point is that in an exchange, you can go into and out of trades very quickly. You don't have to worry about who you are dealing with; you

[5] An Analysis of CDS Transactions: Implications for Public Reporting. Kathryn Chen, Michael Fleming, John Jackson, Ada Li, Asani Sarkar. Federal Reserve Bank of New York Staff Reports (no. 517), September 2011. http://www.newyorkfed.org/research/staff_reports/sr517.pdf.

[6] Transactions are conducted directly between two parties, or off-exchange and without the supervision of an exchange.

don't have to worry about the credit worthiness of your counterparty. It's a very simple trade and the product is highly standardized. The products are very simple. This is unique, based on my study of OCT markets. The OTC market is far more complex. There's lots more complexity in doing a trade.

BROOKS: Can for-profit exchanges still be unique? Can they still offer this degree of confidence, investor protection, and fairness that you all alluded to?

BERKELEY: Sure, the strategic issue that exchanges face today is that, by law, they deal with broker dealers. Broker dealers are often larger economic units than the exchanges. They grew up in a non-profit exchange model in which the exchanges were regarded as utilities, they were there for the public good. The question is, where is the value afforded by the entire process as investors interacts with a trading process that involves broker dealers and exchanges? How is the value of these services divided? As exchanges have become public, and as they have developed their own growth imperatives, the benefit of being public is that they now have the capital to invest, to grow, and to modernize. The disadvantage is that the exchanges now have to make more and more money. That is anathema to the broker community or to the dealer community because they want to be the ones who make that money.[7] So it's a very tough balance of power. We are watching it being fought out in real time.

KATZ: I have lived in both worlds. Twenty-five years ago I worked at an exchange that was then not-for-profit. Later I joined the ISE as a private company that was for-profit.[8] Then the ISE became a public for-profit company. I can tell you from my experience that the way the exchange competes today as a for-profit firm is night and day different. There is no comparison between a publicly-traded exchange focused on building its business and making money, versus an exchange that is operated as a private utility.

The difference is not just the capital used for new technologies and new products. It is also the mindset of the people who work at each kind of company. The types of people you want to attract into the exchange business today are looking for companies they can grow with, and be compensated

[7] With the transformation of exchanges into public companies, the broker dealer community in the U.S. is now competing more directly than before with exchanges for order flow and chasing the same profit opportunities as exchanges. "The broker dealer community now effectively disciplines the exchanges by routing orders away from them," noted one trading expert in a research interview for this book.

[8] Prior to a stint as co-founder and president of K-Square Research, Katz was a managing director at the New York Stock Exchange and worked there from 1986 to 1997.

by. This fight, this balance between the broker dealer and the exchange that you refer to, is real. Yet both of them can win. The broker dealers make money by selling products to their customers, new ETF products or index options, for example. Many of these products are created by the exchanges.

The broker dealers are able to process more trades in which they earn commissions by using technology and systems that the exchanges provide. So there is a healthy balance as they square off against each other, each trying to win a greater piece of the pie. At the same time, the ability of both participants to succeed in this environment has been enhanced by competition. That only happens when the for-profit model is used on both the broker dealer side and the exchange side.

O'BRIEN: I'll echo some of that, and maybe take a slightly different tack. Direct Edge has thought about what an exchange is. We are unique on this panel in that we actively sought and obtained exchange status. We chose to make the transition from operating as an Alternative Trading System to being an exchange.[9] To go back to my original analogy, I think it all stays rooted in whether or not you continue to focus on your user. If you choose to make the transition to the for-profit status you can manage it quite successfully. I don't think exchanges are different from other for-profit businesses in the sense of having to interact with and serve a user community that has significant market power. Whether you are a for-profit or not, you still need to meet the needs of your customers.

I would say, once again, whether it is all Facebook users combined, or every McDonald's customer combined, the users in every case have a collective power that is greater than that of the institution trying to serve them.

I don't think the transition from acting as a utility to trying to make money is the key issue. Exchanges that are operating in a for-profit status, especially public ones, do need a goal. Perhaps it is not simply to make more money, but to grow in a way that people view as sustainable.

REDFEARN: Can a for-profit exchange still convey that confidence to the market? Absolutely, the answer is "yes." Exchanges are still highly regulated entities. Many of the things that inspire confidence are, in part, created by the regulatory framework.

The for-profit issue is more of an economic issue. Exchanges moved away from being membership-type organizations, or the utilities structure, to the for-profit structure. Now there are different incentives involved, in particular there is a greater emphasis today on the creation of shareholder value. During

[9] In July 2010 Direct Edge transitioned to full exchange status having obtained regulatory approval earlier in the same year.

their evolution to this for-profit status, you have also seen the arrival of new startup markets, new venues that now provide valuable competition in the market. This competition helps keep the for-profit incentive in check, as too much of a focus on profitability would inevitably result in a loss of market share to these competitive venues. Some of the participants on this panel today are, or have been, examples of new venues that entered the market to provide competition. Bill O'Brien at Direct Edge, Al Berkeley at Pipeline, and Gary Katz at ISE have all been part of this dynamic.

SARKAR: I want to return to the OTC markets. Let's step ask, why are our OTC markets so complex? They are complex because there is a demand from certain users for more customized products. Maybe you are trading a swap or an option, and you want the contract to expire on a certain date for which a standardized contract is not available. I believe that the demand for customization will become ever greater as users' sophistication grows.

As Bill and Brett mentioned, for-profit exchanges have to respond to the needs of their users. That is why you have this proliferation of new markets and new services. For example, there is a venue for someone who wants to trade a large block of shares with a lower market impact, or for someone else who wants to trade very, very quickly. It is difficult for the exchanges to meet these kinds of specialized needs if they keep their traditional product structure and their traditional, simple market structure. That's where there is this tension—exchanges are trying to meet this need without losing their brand. It will be interesting to see how that trade off and tension will play out.

BROOKS: One of the things that we have learned over the years from Bob's conferences is the importance of innovation. Competition certainly stirs innovation. That said, it has also been pointed out by many that bad outcomes often start out as very good ideas. With an often singular focus on promoting competition in this country, we are now up to something on the order of some 13 stock exchanges.[10] I hear there is an exchange opening on South Beach. I am hoping to visit and ring the opening bell. It could be a lot of fun! [Laughter]. Here's my point: In this environment, perhaps this ruthless kind of competition, or whatever you might want to call it, has caused exchanges to lose some of their uniqueness. They have lost some of their brand, and some of the unique attributes and offerings they might otherwise bring to investors.

[10] There were 13 public exchanges and up to 50 dark pools in the U.S. as of writing in September 2013. That total number of exchanges could change with the pending merger of Direct Edge and BATS, as announced in August 2013, to form the second largest exchange in the U.S.

SARKAR: I see some broader tensions. One is within the business model of an exchange. The exchange needs to reach out to a wide variety of users without hurting its brand and harming traditional users that value its simplicity. That is a business decision that each exchange has to make in terms of how far it can go in the direction of satisfying the needs of more specialized users. It is also interesting that some of these non-exchanges, some of these over-the-counter markets, are in ways becoming more like exchanges. There is a proposal in the Dodd-Frank Act to move some of these products—swaps—to exchange-type systems.[11] Maybe the different paradigms we have today in the OTC and the exchange worlds are moving towards each other and are becoming less different.

From the regulators' viewpoint, what do these kinds of changes do to the stability of the financial system? Do they lead to too much fragmentation? Does this all lead to a reduction of transparency so that regulators' cannot know where the risks are in the system? This evolving issue will play out in the next few years. [12]

REDFEARN: The beauty of our economic system is that competition thrives. Competition in turn helps to stimulate innovation and competitive pricing. I think of the NYSE, a market that has gone from an 80% market share to 20% or so.[13] Does that affect the brand of that market? In some respects, yes. But that is the impact of competition. These are good things, right?

We all remember the debates about competition versus fragmentation when Rule 390 was going away.[14] We had to debate the central limit order

[11] Title VII of the Dodd-Frank Act requires the trading of swaps to occur on Swap Execution Facilities. http://www.law.cornell.edu/wex/dodd-franktitlevii.

[12] It is an evolving issue, explained Sarkar in a subsequent explanation, because the CFTC and SEC must write rules to implement the DFA requirements. "This takes time because the issues are complex and require feedback from industry and the public," he added. "There is a comment period during which anyone can respond/object to aspects of the rules. However, substantial progress has been made, especially with the transparency requirements." See, http://www.mofo.com/files/Uploads/Images/130411-Dodd-Frank-Title-VII-Recent-Developments.pdf.

[13] This refers to market share in the stock trading of NYSE's own listed companies as competition opened up with the enactment of Reg NMS, adopted in 2005, and other regulatory and technological changes.

[14] A former New York Stock Exchange rule that stipulated that, unless exempted by the exchange, members needed permission before trading an exchange-listed security off the exchange floor. Rule 390 was scrapped in 2000 by the NYSE under pressure from the Securities and Exchange Commission.

Source: Wall Street Words: An A to Z Guide to Investment Terms for Today's Investor by David L. Scott.

book back in the day.[15] We needed to move away from a monopolistic environment in order to stimulate competition. Now we are seeing the emergence of more stock exchanges, a large number of dark pools, and liquidity that is far more fragmented today. These are all challenges we are trying to think through.

One could argue that smart order routing,[16] the integration of data feeds, and these sorts of technological innovations have helped to recreate aggregated price discovery and efficient liquidity pools. However, we have to continue to examine the health of our current market structure. Is the level of fragmentation the right level to optimally stimulate innovation and competition? Or, at what point have we taken this competition too far?

O'BRIEN: No, I don't think that competition will impact the ability of exchanges to deliver value to their users. The number of stock exchanges is almost artificial. In fact, Direct Edge, BATS, the NYSE, and NASDAQ account for 99% of all exchange traded bonds in the U.S. The other exchanges operate at the margin. The fact that the larger players operate multiple exchanges is really more a function of market structure regulation because exchanges cannot offer multiple product offerings under a single exchange umbrella.

Our competitors have effectively copied us in a variety of ways. But there is a balance that needs to be struck between the value an individual exchange can provide to its user community, and the collective value that exchanges provide to the financial market community at large. As a group, exchanges need to focus on ensuring investor confidence. That said, market structure regulation does a fairly good job of forcing interaction between the exchanges. For the most part, we are getting better at this.

You may not always get the optimal outcome each time you execute a trade on whatever exchange. But you will get a rational outcome that, at the heart of the market, is the confidence that allows the economy to move forward.

[15] The Central Limit Order Book (CLOB) was a proposal of the National Market Advisory Board (NMAB) in response to the Securities Act amendments of 1975. The NMAB's CLOB would have contained all "declared bids and offers from investors, exchange specialists and over-the-counter market makers, queued and displayed in price-time priority sequence," as part of a national market system. All exchanges were to have been linked to the CLOB, a goal that was later rejected as the Intermarket Trading System (ITS) came into favor.

[16] Smart order routing is the process of electronically routing and obtaining the best available price in trading a security at various liquidity destinations based on price, cost, speed of execution, probability of execution, size and other factors.

KATZ: The growth in the number of exchanges is directly an outcome of exchanges trying to innovate. As Bill correctly pointed out, if an exchange wants to change its matching algorithm, if it wants to change from one model to the next and then have them both at the same time, the only way that's possible for a U.S. exchange is to create an additional exchange. This is why so many exchange groups offer multiple platforms to target different segments of their user community with different pricing and/or market models. The reason behind that is that the SEC does not allow an exchange to have two different rule sets for products they trade. Consequently, you literally have to create another exchange.

By definition, proliferation is because of innovation. Each exchange is trying to adjust its model and test different approaches to pricing. Different market structures help grow the business. There are two different types of innovation. There are new products, and you don't need a new exchange to create a new product. But if you want to tweak your model just a little bit, regulation requires that you need another exchange. This has been good for the customer. In the options industry, we have seen the growth of exchanges. We are now up to nine.[17] Each new exchange has caused the other industry participants to step up their game, to develop better technology, to create better pricing for the customer, along with more transparency and more products. Competition, as measured by the number of exchanges, is an indication that innovation is alive and well.

BERKELEY: Here are some interesting observations from a macroeconomics perspective. There is enough capacity in the exchange business, and in the alternative trading system business, to satisfy all the demands for trading—many, many times over. Innovation needs to be both in the processes and in the selection of the customer base. The fundamental problem that institutional investors face is how to efficiently move large quantities of stock in and out of the marketplace at the best possible prices. This problem has not yet been solved, but it is very close. The innovation is happening because people continue to think that new rules of engagement will allow them to operate more profitably.

We think that the move to predictive analytics[18] is a fundamentally important break in the way services are offered to investors. The introduction

[17] With the introduction of Gemini in August 2013, the U.S. had 12 U.S. options exchanges, according to the Street.com.

[18] "Predictive analytics describes a range of analytical and statistical techniques used for developing models that may be used to predict future events or behaviors. There are different forms of predictive models, which vary based on the event or behavior that is being predicted. Nearly all predictive models produce a score; a higher score indicates that

of predicative analytics forces you to choose between optimizing your exchange for liquidity providers and liquidity users. I strongly agree that competition is good. It is indicative of an effort to innovate. But it is important to recognize that the game continues to change.

BROOKS: Mr. Price, the founder of T Rowe Price, once said that change is an investor's only certainty. That assertion is probably as true today as it was back then. But let's see if we can tone this rhetoric up a touch. You know, depending on the day, you might read that high-frequency trading accounts for 75% of the stock exchange volume, that the average trade execution size is 140 or 200 shares or something.[19] Some institutional volume is certainly being broken up into a million little trades to access the market. There is also, perhaps, a lot of other kinds of trading. Exchanges have multiple constituencies to serve. The challenge is to serve everybody with fairness and with some sense of confidence. How do you do this in an environment where high- frequency trading is potentially that big, and where the incentives to route order flow can be dictated by some perverse economic incentive[20] How do we find some common ground? Or, how do we find balance, if you will?

Many investors feel that their confidence in markets and the pricing process is severely challenged. Many investors don't understand what's going on. And yet volume growth is necessary for the exchanges. They are predicated on growing volume. So where do we find common ground there? What needs to be reasserted to promote what an exchange historically has uniquely offered?

BERKELEY: I would like everybody in the room to blink their eyes. Did everybody blink? Depending on the twitch speed of your muscles, your blink took between 50 and 150 milliseconds. A modern trading system can trade up to five times in that period. Every trade involves several steps: To observe the market conditions; to orient that to a historical database; to decide whether to act or not; to send in the order; and to get the execution. It is very difficult for human beings to compete with that today.

a given event or behavior is very likely to occur. Predictive analytics, along with data mining techniques and predictive models, relies on multivariate analyzing techniques, including time-series or advanced regression models. These techniques allow organizations to decide on relationships and trends and predict future behaviors or events." Source: Techopedia.

[19] See, Cracks in the Pipeline, Part Two. High Frequency Trading. Wallace C. Turbeville, *Demos*, March 2013.http://www.demos.org/publication/cracks-pipeline-part-two-high-frequency-trading.

[20] In a subsequent interview, Brooks included rebates paid to customers for routing their orders to a specific execution venue as a "perverse" economic incentive.

At the same time, I don't think that any of us want to say that we are living back in 1848 when this new unfair technology called the telegraph was introduced. None of us want to say that people who have telegraphs are somehow getting an unfair advantage over people who still use horses! The right answer is to let the rules of engagement evolve. If an advance in technology has an unintended consequence, or if it presents a set of advantages to the people who possess it, then in a modern, free market you can either acquire those capabilities, or you can have an intermediary emerge with rules of engagement that somehow create a more level playing field. You can indeed compete and make it more difficult for a technological advance to take competitive advantage of you.

KATZ: It's funny. When I blinked my eyes, all I could think of was my father banging on the door of the room saying, "When are you going to get off the telephone? You have been on the phone for 4 hours!" I've got four kids. I never bang on their doors anymore because they are on the phone. Instead, they are on the Internet, listening to music, chatting with their friends and using up none of my phone bill.

We are living in a completely different world than what many of us here today grew up in 30 or 40 years ago. It is even so very different than the world we knew 10 years ago. When ISE launched in 2000, the reason we couldn't come to market 2 years before that was because the modem speed was too low.

I am not going to tell you how many trades we can do in 150 milliseconds. You would be shocked. But that's the world that we are living in today. That is the marketplace as we know it today. But let me ask you to blink for a moment and think about the experience you have as a trader today. You get instantaneous executions. You know exactly what your portfolio's value is at any moment in time. You have Internet sites that give you data on options, futures, and stock, instantaneously during the day, 24 h a day, and even over the weekend. By historical standards, you have the lowest commissions that have ever been charged to you as a customer. You have access to products globally because of the structures that have been created. It doesn't mean that you should ever stop trying to find a level playing field.

Change is a continuous process, it is an evolution. It requires regulators who understand the marketplace and are engaged with the exchanges and broker dealers. It is a never ending process. It is one that we should not try to move back from. We need to continue to move forward and embrace the technology that is available to us.

O'BRIEN: I have no plans to ask anyone to blink, first and foremost. (Laughter)

BROOKS: We do it automatically, actually!

O'BRIEN: Andy, I keep hearing institutions complaining about the decrease in the average trade size. There is a plan in place that if stock prices continue to go down, we are going to get that trade size way up because every stock will be trading for under a dollar per share. Isn't that great! Please, I am only joking! (Laughter)

BROOKS: We were hoping it wouldn't happen that way.

O'BRIEN: I don't think an increase in the average trade size is necessarily reflective of a healthier market. As regards the HFT level playing field, a lot of that criticism is unfair and poorly cast, especially in times of financial markets stress. People have a love-hate relationship with the stock market and financial markets generally.

You can read critical statements about speculators in the New York newspapers back in the 1920's, and in the London newspapers as far back as the 1820's, and in the Dutch newspapers even further back in the 1620's. Only the jargon in each period is different. We can do a better job on some of the things exchanges can uniquely do. One is education. That is a key difference in the role that an exchange as distinct from a trading system can play.

In that sense, options systems are better today than the stock markets—they focus more on product awareness and education. Everyone in this room knows how much better off you are with today's stock market than people were with the stock market 10 or 20 years ago. But that message hasn't been communicated well to the average American.

Exchanges put a lot more effort into investor education today than they did 10–20 years ago. Exchanges need to educate their customers, not with the intention of making them captive to their legacy brands or legacy perceptions, but to make sure that traders and investors know about where every type of market participant fits in global financial markets. That is in everyone's long term interest.

We at Direct Edge are in the middle of this user community. We have a good insight into where participants would like to see the financial markets heading. At Direct Edge, I am honored to talk in a single day with proprietary trading firms such as Goldman Sachs, Fidelity, Scottrade, and the likes of TD Ameritrade. That gives us insight that we need to share in a productive and collaborative way with regulators and other stakeholders. We want to make sure that confidence stays vibrant going forward. Finally, we should never lose sight of the fact that we are also a self-regulatory organization.

That is another thing that makes an exchange unique. We police member conduct. Focusing on conduct more than on capabilities is a much more prudent and, frankly, rational way to go. At Direct Edge we are taking that responsibility very seriously. We are investing more time and talent than we ever have before. If exchanges fill their role in those regards—and maybe if the indexes go up and assist us a little bit—then some of the things that we are so concerned about today will start to recede.

REDFEARN: If we asked everyone in the audience to define high-frequency trading, you would be amazed at the possible number of answers we would get. I can't necessarily define it, except to say that it would include the activities and the participants who are trying to trade really fast and at a high frequency. These could include our broker algorithmic customer business; statistical arbitrage; electronic market making and other proprietary trading activities in the market. Just about everybody in today's electronic markets is trying to trade fast because it is a very fast market environment.

Some of the numbers being thrown about in terms of the HFT percentage of the market are fairly suspect. Certainly, it is hard to give an exact number when we can't exactly define what we are giving a number for. Regardless, I don't know of another category of trader that is so widely scapegoated for so many of today's markets ills.

What are we trying to understand about the markets today? That's what we should ask. And some of those questions are: What are the different sources of order flow that are causing volatility in the markets? Is it the participants, for example, the high-frequency traders; is it the type of strategy, for example, opportunistic and/or, is it certain types of products that are traded in the marketplace, for example, leveraged ETFs?

What is the short-term liquidity provision model that we have today? We don't have the New York Stock Exchange specialists as we did before the introduction of Reg NMS in 2005.[21] With its new technology and its new rules, the NASDAQ market maker world has changed completely. And here is another question: How should we slow down or stop the markets when volatility gets out of control, when things are moving too fast? Some of the regulatory responses to that include single stock circuit breakers, limit up, limit down,[22] or things like that. In my view, focusing on fundamental questions and issues is far more important than coming up with an ill-defined category like HFT and then trying to figure out what they are doing that is creating all these problems.

[21] See, Final rules and amendments to joint industry plans. http://www.sec.gov/rules/final/34-51808.pdf.

[22] As of September 2013, the limit-up/limit-down system had replaced the circuit breakers which would temporary halt or pause trading based on certain price range parameters. The limit-up/limit down system was advanced by regulators in response to wild swings in securities, in particular the May 2010 Flash Crash that briefly sent the Dow Jones Industrial Average tumbling down almost 1,000 points.

SARKAR: High-frequency trading is a set of innovations that responded to the apparent need of certain users for very, very rapid trading. If you are in a competitive marketplace, it's very difficult to say I want this set of innovations but I don't want this other type of innovation. So, in that sense, high-frequency trading is here, and the question is, how do we understand it? How do we deal with it? And the most important question about high-frequency trading, or any other type of innovation, is what are the natural effects of these innovations? What are the effects of the innovations that make some people feel uncomfortable? How is HFT affecting the more regular types of trading?

If you look at what some of these high-frequency trading firms are doing, some of these activities are indeed hard to understand. We have these very rapid cancellations. We have these computers that are sending out very high-frequency orders that are being cancelled in milliseconds. What is the purpose of that? What's going on here? I haven't seen anything that explains the purpose of these strategies. It goes back to something that Bill and Brett were saying- education is very important. First, there is education in terms of research to understand what these high-frequency traders are doing. Second, when these HFT guys trade, how does it impact the marketplace in general? We need to look at the interaction between the market price and these orders, and when these orders are coming into the marketsplace; what's happening with liquidity, price impact, and volatility, etc.? It is hard to recommend any kind of policy or enforcement. Frankly, we do not have a good understanding at all of what high-frequency trading is, and of what its impact on the market is.

BROOKS: You all touched on two things that are most interesting. One is the concept of education; and the other is the concept of enforcement. If we don't understand some of the things happening in the marketplace today, then clearly exchanges and others have an obligation to educate investors on the different products, on the good things that come from them, and perhaps on the things that need to be addressed.

Then we come to the enforcement side. There is the issue of huge cancellation rates, and seemingly not only rebate arbitrage but market data arbitrage on top of that! [23] That leads people to feel that perhaps the game isn't fair because someone is getting an edge—not because of hard work, but because of something else. How do we address that? How do we say, gee, you know we have done this, but it's not very fair. Let's pull back a bit. Any

[23] What to Do about High-Frequency Trading. Rodney Sullivan, CFA. *CFA Institute*, 24 April, 2013) http://blogs.cfainstitute.org/investor/2013/04/24/what-to-do-about-high-frequency-trading/.

thoughts on what we might be able to do as an industry to help educate the public and the regulators? The regulators certainly need to understand what's happening in this market as well.

REDFEARN: Why are there so many order cancellations, and why is everything moving so fast in the market? Let me mention a recent and interesting speech made at the SIFMA conference in 2011 by Gregg Berman who is at the SEC's Division of Trading and Markets.[24] Gregg talked about various forms of arbitrage in the market. In particular, he noted how ETFs are a very significant percentage of the market today, especially SPDRS and the triple Q.[25] Think about the pricing of an underlying ETF. When your aunt or uncle is buying an ETF, he or she would like to be confident that they are buying at the right price. The way that pricing happens for an exchange traded fund is often based upon an arbitrage that exists with the underlying basket of securities that make up that EFT, as well as the related futures product. The participants who are engaging in these index arbitrage practices—consequently, the ones who are keeping the prices of the ETF in line—are effectively doing many of the actions well understood to be HFT, in particular very fast trading with frequent order cancellations. This is what Gregg Berman was talking about. Let me be clear: a market participant engaging in index arbitrage may be trading in an underlying basket of stocks, and the related product in the futures market, removing pricing inefficiencies and thereby ensuring that the ETF is priced accurately. So that when your Aunt and Uncle go out and buy SPY,[26] they're getting the right price. I am not saying that all market participants who have extremely low order-to-trade ratios—that is, are cancelling many orders per trade—are adding necessary efficiencies to the marketplace. But with fast trading and high cancellation rates, it is important that we do not start with an assumption that, in and of itself, these practices are bad for today's marketplace.

O'BRIEN: I always struggle with the notion of fairness. I segment concerns into fair and unfair concerns. The unfair concerns today are usually from people such as some market structure critics who are not directly

[24] Market Structure: What we Know, and What we Need to Know. Presented by Gregg E. Berman 12th Annual SIFMA Market Structure Conference September 21, 2011, New York. Berman was a Senior Advisor to the Director, Division of Trading and Markets at the SEC.
See, http://www.sifma.org/uploadedfiles/events/2011/market_structure/berman-remarks.pdf?n=38285.

[25] SPDR funds are a family of exchange-traded funds (ETFs) managed by State Street Global Advisors. QQQ's, or Triple Q's are an ETF, enabling an investor to purchase the entire NASDAQ 100 Index via a single security.

[26] SPDR S&P 500 Trust ETF (SPY).

affiliated with an exchange. They think a lot of things aren't fair. I don't think they are worried about whether or not someone is trading. They have a much broader sense of fairness concerns, and they may or may not be valid. They are really not talking about high-frequency trading. But fairness has to start with an understanding, and it's driven by the conduct of market participants more so than their capabilities.

The average retail investor is not looking to arb the futures versus the underlying. It's not a matter of, so and so has a higher-speed line, or they're collocated, so they beat me to the punch.[27] Usually those people are interacting on other sides of the trade when you are buying the SPY to hold for a relativity long period of time. You are interacting with a short-term trader, and that interaction is not one where you are a winner or a looser. You are both beneficiaries.

Once again, this is what makes exchanges unique. Bringing buyers and seller together in a way that benefits both parties. The fact that they have different objectives and different capabilities is not fundamentally unfair. I don't understand anyone who implies that it is. That said, it is true that the transformation of how trades take place on exchanges means that we have a similar responsibility to advance our capabilities to understand what is happening on exchanges.

BROOKS: I agree.

O'BRIEN: You see a host of initiatives that, although perhaps a bit overdue, are advancing our marketplace for the better. These initiatives include the consolidated audit trail, and Large Trader Reporting.[28] I am not commenting or wholeheartedly endorsing the fine details of each of these initiatives. I think their spirit and the focus is appropriate, so that we match

[27] O'Brien is referring to how Wall Street trading firms place, or co-locate, their trading computers in the same data centers as an exchange's for the purposes of having the fastest possible access to exchange market data. This practice gives trading firms an edge over other investors who access the same data at slower speeds from a consolidated feed of data, critics contend.

[28] On July 11, 2012, the U.S. Securities and Exchange Commission adopted Rule 613 under Regulation NMS requiring the national securities exchanges and national securities associations to submit a plan to the SEC to create, implement, and maintain the consolidated audit trail (CAT). The system would not be introduced as early as initially scheduled as exchanges and industry regulator, the Securities Industry and Financial Markets Association, said they would submit their plans by December 2013, a full 8 months later than originally scheduled.

For more on CAT and Large Trader Reporting, which was approved in 2011. See, Sifma Urges End to Some Data Systems as Audit Trail Nears. Nina Mehta, *Bloomberg,* March 28, 2013. http://www.bloomberg.com/news/2013-03-28/sifma-urges-end-to-some-data-systems-as-audit-trail-approaches.html.

our technological and product innovation with our regulatory innovation, and keep pace in that regard. If you do that, you can start to prosecute people who are using new technologies to effectuate what are probably some of the oldest schemes in the book. Then the fairness concerns, or at least the rational ones, start to fall away.

BROOKS: Some questions from the attendees?

GEORGE SELINSKY (Baruch College MBA student): Will there ever be a need for a 24-h equities market like we have in the currency market?

BROOKS: No and No! (Laughter): Just a selfish response, sorry. Anyone?

O'BRIEN: If users want it yes. If they don't, no. Our trading system at Direct Edge is so flexible that we can keep it open all day. Why don't we just do it? Will people come?

REDFEARN: I frequently travel around the country and speak to institutional money managers. I remember when the NYSE was talking about extending the trading day by opening the market an hour earlier. When I would discuss this possibility with clients in San Francisco and LA, they looked at me cross-eyed. Of course, meetings with West Coast clients were often held around 5:00 AM Pacific time. Given the 3 h time difference between the East and West Coasts, clients on the West Coast would look at me and say, "Please don't let them ever do that because that's just not going to work here."

In the equity markets, for a trade to occur, two or more orders need to meet at the same price and in the same place. The reason why we have big prints and so much trading around the open and close is that liquidity aggregates during those points in time in particular. When I talk about fragmentation, I think of fragmentation in three dimensions: place, price and time. When we went to decimal pricing, we fragmented price. With so many exchanges and over 40 dark pools, we've fragmented place. And when markets were automated, we fragmented time.

At the NYSE less than 10 years ago, the turnaround time for the execution of a market order was often over a minute. As markets automated, trading speeds went to seconds, then sub-seconds, milliseconds, and now microseconds. With that we fragmented time. Today, the ability for orders to aggregate and for liquidity to meet at the same point in time is actually more challenging. This also helps to explain why we have such lower market depth and smaller trade sizes than we once did. With the significant increase in the speed of the market and the fragmentation of time, we effectively expanded the trading day because we exponentially increased the number of possible increments of time during which a trade could take place.

BOB O'BRIEN: (KCI Technologies): Since you have hinted that a lot of the trading is virtual trading, how do you separate the regulation of virtual trading from the regulation of real trading so that you can better monitor the market?

BROOKS: What do you mean by virtual market?

BOB O'BRIEN: You said that a lot of trades get busted.

BROOKS: Do you mean that quotes get canceled?

BOB O'BRIEN: Yes, I call it virtual trading. It is not real trading. So separate that from the real trading. How do you go after virtual trading from a regulatory perspective?

SARKAR: As I mentioned earlier, it is hard to say what to do about that if you don't understand why these things are being done. What is the real purpose behind the people who are doing this? We first have to understand the logic behind this and the impact that this is having on the market. Only then can you talk about whether it's necessary to regulate.

REDFEARN: There is obviously a lot of concern with the amount of message traffic that's in the market. A bit earlier I provided an example of where certain market participants with high order-to trade ratios contribute to efficient price discovery. But that example doesn't mean that all participants with high cancellation rates are contributing to market efficiencies and are playing by the rules. For instance, we have rules against "spoofing" the market, and regulations prohibiting "layering" strategies.[29] Both of these strategies can utilize opportunistic quoting techniques where quotes that are being placed in the market are not reflective of the prices at which the quoting participant actually wants to trade. If someone is using trading strategies that violate existing regulations, then by all means let's hope that the regulators are seeing this and are properly enforcing against these activities.

The key is that there are some cases where there are legitimate strategies that fall under the category of HFT. There are some cases where trading is based on paired securities or multiple securities that tend to move in relationship to one another, in a statistically defined manner. Some of these trading strategies cancel a lot simply due to the speed at which the prices of the related securities are changing, and these strategies may provide pricing efficiencies to the market. Then, there are other strategies that may

[29] Layering is the practice by traders of placing multiple, often large, orders that are not intended to be executed and which are then quickly cancelled. The idea is to create artificial levels of supply and demand, driving the price of stock artificially up or down, at which point "legitimate" orders are completed to make money from the inflated or reduced price. Spoofing is where traders also place multiple, non-legitimate orders to create false selling or buying interest in stocks to garner advantageous prices.

be manipulative or in violation of some rule. In this case, it is important that existing regulations be enforced to curtail inappropriate behaviors. We need to understand these variations among types of HFT participants before we rush to impose new regulations on anything HFT.

BERKELEY: It is also worth pointing out that the lifespan of an order is one of those rules of engagement that could be offered in a different way through innovation. You would have to see whether people would like to go to a market that had a required life of an order.[30] Right now you can cancel an order as fast as you want.

BROOKS: As you can tell from this excellent discussion, we need to demystify some of the things in the market. We have to encourage enforcement. We need to encourage education and reaffirm that sense of fairness that all of our markets and all of our business frankly depend on. Please join me in thanking this wonderful panel!

[30] Berkeley was referring to the idea of having orders that are available for a specific period of time, say 5 s or 2 s, rather than mere microseconds as is the case today with a market structure that permits flickering quotes and traders to cancel an order as fast as they are practically able. As of this writing, this is a matter that the Securities and Exchange Commission was watching with an eye towards extending the lifespan of an order.

CHAPTER 3: MID-DAY ADDRESS: THE MODERN EXCHANGE ORGANIZATION

Reto Francioni, *CEO, Deutsche Börse AG*

I would like to share my thoughts on three fundamental themes of exchange organizations[1]:

First, in a globalized economy, exchange organizations must be global in both their services and their operations. Their role is to organize safe and orderly markets that deliver efficient price discovery to the benefit of the national, supranational and international economies—and this is a global public good. This can only be carried out by a regulated, highly transparent exchange organization.

Second, price discovery is increasingly being supplemented by further services aimed especially at risk management. This is reflected in the growing trend of exchange organizations to become integrated infrastructure providers, as well as by current legislative initiatives in the US and in the EU.

Third, the dual role of exchange organizations as global providers of price discovery and risk management services is verified by the recent strong increases in exchange order book volumes as a consequence of market turbulence. Regulated exchange organizations are anchors of stability in times of increasing volatility.

GLOBALIZATION

What are the classical functions of an exchange? Regulated exchange organizations provide the infrastructure that makes markets work. First of all, they contribute to economic growth by providing access to capital markets for companies in the real economy. An exchange brings buyers and sellers together, concentrates their orders, and executes deals on liquid

[1] Please note that this chapter reflects market conditions prevailing during the time this speech was made by Reto Francioni. Moreover, it has not been updated since to account for changes in market conditions.

R.A. Schwartz et al. (eds.), *The Economic Function of a Stock Exchange*, Zicklin School of Business Financial Markets Series, DOI 10.1007/978-3-319-10350-1_3

and transparent markets. By creating conditions for liquidity provision and transparency, they discover market prices. And by discovering prices, they provide an important service to the economy as a whole: Well discovered market prices are the best guarantee that capital will be put where it is needed most (Exhibit 3.1).

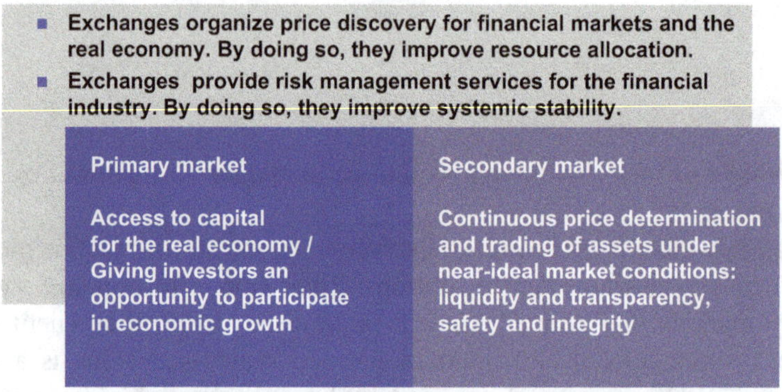

Exhibit 3.1 What does an exchange do?

By implication, exchange organizations are also useful for regulators who are concerned with protecting investors, improving the functioning of markets, and reducing systemic risks. In the past, regulators performed these functions for their home country only. At present—and the need will be even greater in the future—regulators need to coordinate internationally. In Europe, we see a clear trend in this direction: New EU supervisory authorities have been set up to improve supervisory structures. For example, the European Securities and Markets Authority, ESMA,[2] directly supervises service providers in the securities industry and develops guidelines for their regulation.

Exchange organizations with global reach will be well positioned to work with international regulators to facilitate transparency and the standardization of the global markets, while at the same time preserving national regulatory models. They can serve as natural partners for harmonization and transparency across jurisdictions.

Our work at Deutsche Börse[3] has changed because the work of exchange organizations itself has undergone an impressive and far-reaching transformation over the past 20 years. These changes have been driven by advances

[2] See http://www.esma.europa.eu.

[3] See http://www.deutsche-boerse.com.

in technology that have cut costs and increased the speed of trading as well as transparency and market integrity. Regulation like the EUs Markets in Financial Instruments Directive—in short, known as MiFID[4]—have spurred these changes. Changes have also been caused by competition, especially from new niche players on the markets, as well as by internationally established exchange organizations.

In response, this change has triggered a wave of consolidation among established exchange organizations. Consequently, fewer exchange organizations now span more markets and products. It has become a strategic necessity that, in a global economy, exchange organizations must become global as well. It's not enough to focus on home markets. We have to expand and seek new partners to secure our position.

Change is also increasingly being demanded by our clients. Furthermore, the technology being deployed for equities and derivatives trading demand continual investments to attract low-latency trading flow, so the ability to make these offerings scalable through consolidation makes much sense from a cost perspective.

There will soon be a very limited number of really global and highly professional exchange organizations. That is my personal scenario for the near future of the exchange world. These exchange organizations will cover a broad range of financial instruments and infrastructure services. They will be in fierce competition with each other and, at the same time, they will open up new opportunities for new niche players. These new players, at the other end of the spectrum, will specialize in certain customer groups or security types (Exhibit 3.2).

The proposed merger between NYSE Euronext and Deutsche Börse[5] has sometimes falsely been portrayed as a story of "Americans" against "Germans" (and vice versa). From a customer perspective, however, things look entirely different. The two most important business areas of Deutsche Börse Group already derive the majority of their sales revenues from outside of Germany: Eurex,[6] our derivatives subsidiary, generates more than two thirds of its revenues from non-German Europe, and a further fifth from the

[4] The Markets in Financial Instruments Directive, or MiFID, was officially enacted on November 1, 2007. The goal is to integrate the European Union's financial markets and to increase the amount of cross-border investment orders. See http://www.sec.gov/about/laws/wallstreetreform-cpa.pdf.

[5] On 1 December 2013, the European Commission announced that it was prohibiting the planned merger between Deutsche Börse AG and NYSE Euronext because, based on its definition of the market for derivatives trading, it considered the merger to be inadmissible under competition law.

[6] See http://www.eurexchange.com.

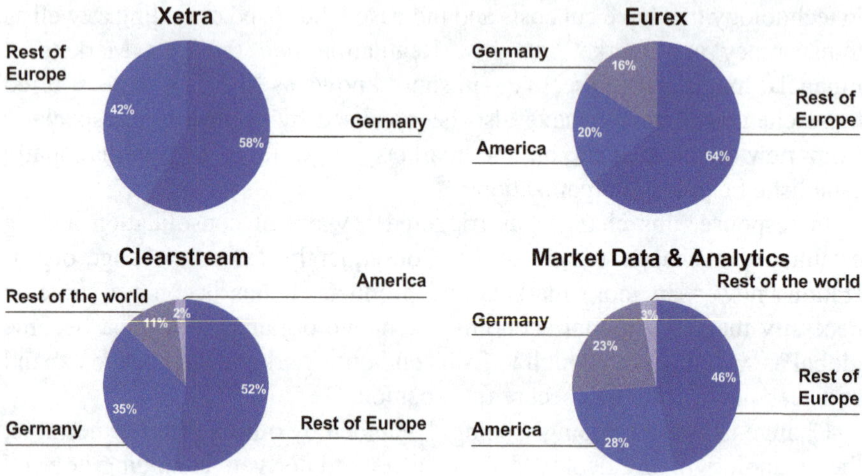

Exhibit 3.2 2010 Sales revenue of Deutsche Börse Group: European, transatlantic, global etc

US. Clearstream,[7] our Luxembourg-based settlement and custody service provider, derives two thirds of its revenues from outside Germany—worldwide. And even Xetra,[8] our electronic stock market, has more than 40% of its revenues coming from outside Germany (although it is confined to giving access to participants residing in Europe for legal reasons) (Exhibit 3.3).

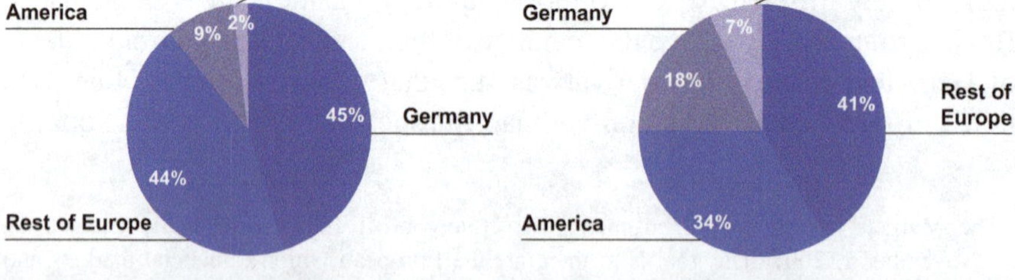

Exhibit 3.3 Deutsche Börse Group: a global network of employees owned by a global network of shareholders

[7] See http://www.clearstream.com.

[8] See http://www.xetra.com.

The same is true from an ownership point of view. Less than one fifth of our owners are German, more than one third are American, and the rest comes from all over the world. In other words, Deutsche Börse already almost a global exchange. The proposed merger with NYSE Euronext will make the two of us together the most international exchange organization there is. This will provide us with an excellent basis to become truly global in the near future.

What is equally clear, however, is that in this globalized exchange world, financial centers such as New York and Frankfurt will continue to matter. Exchange trading is not only about electronic networks; it is also about networks of people. It is about creating communities that are brought together by exchange organizations. Exchange organizations continue to form the nucleus of flourishing financial centers and truly global cities. If we succeed in bringing together the capital market communities in New York and Frankfurt by creating the world's largest exchange organization, then I am sure that this will be to the mutual benefit of both cities. By bundling our technologies, and by making our markets accessible to customers on both sides of the Atlantic and beyond, we will improve liquidity and broaden the range of services we can offer.

RISK MANAGEMENT

Non-transparent markets, and non-transparent products, were at the heart of the financial crisis. Had there been greater transparency, unsustainable risk-return profiles would have become clear to customers, to analysts, and to regulators ex ante,[9] and so the bubble that burst would not have had a great chance to build up in the first place. Conversely, the crisis has shown that, with their transparent and highly regulated markets, exchange organizations can make a valuable contribution towards stabilizing the financial system (Exhibit 3.4).

Exchange organizations have been able at all times to guarantee orderly trading and, therefore, to help ensure transparent price formation. In addition, the central counterparties (CCPs) affiliated with the stock exchanges, such as Eurex Clearing[10] in the case of Deutsche Börse, interpose themselves between counterparties to financial transactions. By doing so, they become

[9] That is to say, heightened transparency would have given a clearer view of such risk profiles before the financial crisis had time to occur.

[10] See http://www.eurexchange.com.

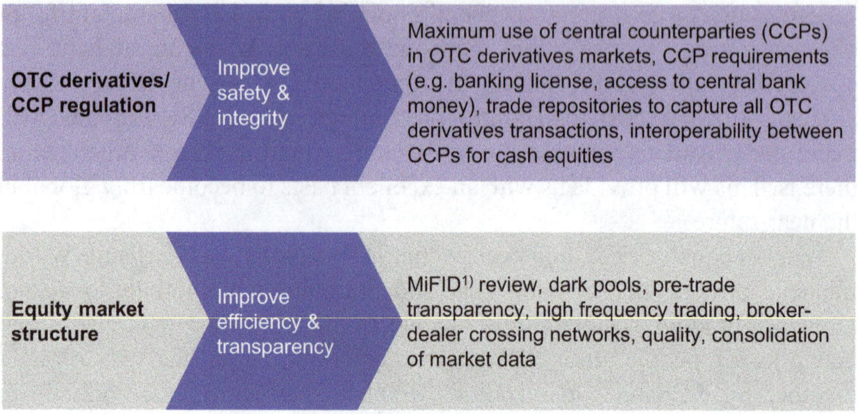

1) MiFID: Markets in Financial Instruments Directive

Exhibit 3.4 Core policy initiatives underway: more safety and integrity for OTC derivatives, more efficiency and transparency for equities

the buyer for the seller and the seller for the buyer. At the same time, they call for collateral geared to individual risk exposure. In this way, CCPs safeguard trading against counterparty risk.

This risk control has also been recognized by political leaders worldwide. In response to the financial crisis, leaders of the twenty largest economies of the world in their G20[11] summits following the financial crisis, have developed proposals for global standards regarding financial market reform. One key recommendation that was made by G20 was the proposal, where appropriate, to migrate OTC derivatives to central market infrastructures. Such infrastructures include organized and supervised forms of trading and CCP clearing.

In the US, the Dodd-Frank Act[12] has been used as the legal vehicle to enact these reforms. Formulating implementation measures regarding OTC derivatives trading is still in progress. In Europe, legislators have used the scheduled revision of MiFID for proposing additional transparency requirements for financial instruments that are traded mostly OTC.

[11] See http://www.g20.org/.

[12] The Dodd-Frank Wall Street Reform and Consumer Protection Act, enacted by the United States Congress, became effective on July 2010. See http://www.sec.gov/about/laws/wallstreetreform-cpa.pdf.

MiFID AND MARKET TRANSPARENCY

MiFID contains pre- and post-trade transparency rules for equities with a clear objective: better achieve fair competition and investor protection. After nearly 4 years of experience, however, we need to admit today that, despite the transparency and reporting requirements under MiFID, we know less about market structures than we did before. The share of OTC trading is growing across Europe, and this trading is taking place outside the transparency rules for organized markets. This results in a lack of transparency, and it discriminates not only against smaller market participants and private investors, but also against the more sophisticated institutional investors, as demonstrated by the financial markets crisis.

In addition, pre- and post-trade transparency is essential for central clearing. Robust post-trade processes rely on transparency. And, as the market practice in clearing moves towards real-time risk management (as offered by Eurex Clearing only), real-time transparency is needed to perform real-time risk management. Therefore, from a trading and clearing perspective, we appreciate an extension of the transparency obligations to non-equity markets (Exhibit 3.5).

Lines of defense clearing house

1. Liquidation of open positions
   Close-out of positions results in surplus or shortfall
2. Liquidation of collateral
   Collateral is liquidated to cover potential shortfalls
3. Guarantee fund contribution of member in default
   Contribution of €1 million to €100 million
4. Reserves of Eurex Clearing
   ~€5 million
5. Guarantee fund contribution of all members
   Clearing fund contribution of other members ~€1bn
6. Liable equity of Eurex Clearing
   ~€110 million
7. Parental Guarantee to Eurex Clearing
   €700 million by Deutsche Börse

€47 billion total guarantee position[1)]

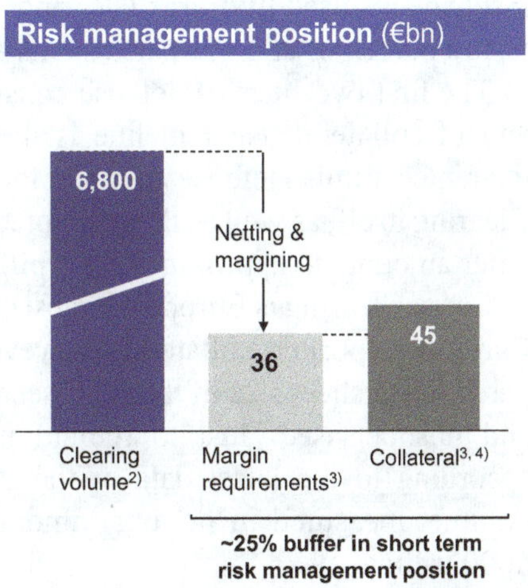

1) Not considering the liquidation of defaulting member's open positions
2) Monthly average April 2009 – March 2010
3) 31 March 2010
4) Cash and securities collateral after haircut, cash collateral ~7% of total

Exhibit 3.5 Counterparty risk at Eurex Clearing effectively managed by collateralization and multiple lines of defense

In other words: Exchange organizations are not at the root of this crisis. On the contrary, we have continued to organize and to maintain regulated, safe, and orderly markets even in the worst of turbulence. Our transparency, safety, and integrity is now widely seen as a remedy against the excessive risk-taking that led to the crisis. At Deutsche Börse Group, we have in addition developed new solutions that help keep the markets going even when liquidity has nearly dried up.

Even the fiercest critics of so-called "vertical silos", i.e., companies such as Deutsche Börse Group which offer the complete value-added chain, today seem to have turned into fans of this type of integration.

And I would therefore propose to finally abandon the pejorative term "vertical silo" and replace it by "integrated exchange," for such an exchange will improve safety and integrity for its clients. Risk management is at the core of the exchange business. Thanks to an integrated approach, exchange organizations like Deutsche Börse are able to offer, for both our customers and our regulators, new innovative and integrated products for better risk management. This does not mean, however, that we should not discuss making access to clearing easier for potential new customers. Integration and accessibility are not mutually exclusive.

Our central counterparty for off-exchange derivatives, which was developed by Eurex Clearing, set in place an effective insurance against counterparty risk, starting with credit default swaps. Here is a taste of the safety mechanisms used by Eurex Clearing: We employ several lines of defense to insure ourselves and our participants against the case of a member's default.

The first two lines of defense consist of the liquidation of open positions and of collateral. Next in line is the contribution of each member to the guarantee fund. Defense number four and five are the reserves of Eurex Clearing itself, as well as the guarantee fund contribution of all members. The latter amounts to approximately 1 billion Euros.

Eurex Clearing is Europe's largest clearing house with more than 40 billion Euros of deposited collateral. However, Eurex Clearing is very small compared to the sheer size of the OTC sector that so far is completely unregulated and unsupervised. Just to remind you of the magnitude of this sector: according to the latest data of the Bank for International Settlements, its volume, measured in notional amounts outstanding, was a staggering US $600 trillion.

Again, do not get me wrong, this sector certainly has its functions. For example, it provides flexible hedging mechanisms to risks taken by globally operating industrial companies. However, as the financial crisis has shown, it can also encourage excess risk taking due to a systematic lack of information about risk, and due to insufficient insurance mechanisms. This is why policy makers need to act. They must make the reform of this sector a top priority—and indeed a higher priority than attempts aimed at additional de-regulation. The paradigm of ideologically-driven de-regulation without any regard for increasing risk, conflicts of interest, and lack of transparency urgently needs to be replaced by a new emphasis on re-establishing safety and integrity.

Neutrality is one of our key strengths when formulating such solutions. We do not have to *manage* conflicts of interest. We *avoid* conflicts of interest vis-à-vis our customers.[13] Therefore, exchange organizations that provide not only trading platforms, but also post-trade infrastructure and market data services as well, are in a unique position to contribute to a sophisticated form of re-regulation of capital markets in Europe. I am not suggesting over-regulation that stifles innovation, but smart regulation that increases the global competitiveness of the European economy. Because this is what capital markets are ultimately there for—to give the real economy access to sorely needed equity capital, and to provide investors with fair, transparent, and reliable investment opportunities.

VOLATILITY

In volatile times, we regularly observe that market participants restructure their portfolios via exchange organizations, and not via OTC trading platforms, because only exchange organizations provide safe, transparent and reliable trading venues. Apart from robust electronic trading and post-trading systems for regulated and supervised markets, the insurance against counterparty risk via CCPs plays an important role. This applies both to stock markets and to derivatives markets.

In August 2011, order volume on Xetra, Deutsche Börse's electronic stock exchange, more than doubled to 182 billion Euros compared to the same month last year. And Eurex, the derivatives exchange, recorded an average daily volume of 13.2 million contracts, an increase of 69%. Of these contracts, 9.1 million were Eurex Exchange contracts, and 4.1 million were traded at the New-York-based International Securities Exchange (ISE), a Eurex subsidiary. Other exchange organizations around the globe experienced similar increases.

In parallel, we see a strong increase in volatility that has continued until September 2011. At Deutsche Börse, we measure implicit volatility through the volatility index, VDAX.[14] It measures the degree of variation that is

[13] Deutsche Börse does not act in the market as a buyer or seller unlike, for example, the sell-side.

[14] DAX is the acronym for "Deutscher Aktienindex" (German exchange index), the German blue chip index containing the 30 leading stocks of the German stock market. For more on VDAX. See http://deutsche-boerse.com/dbg/dispatch/en/kir/dbg_nav/about_us/30_Services/40_Know_how/10_Stock_Exchange_A_Z?glossaryWord=pi_glos_vdax.

expected by the derivatives markets for the coming 30 days. Whereas the VDAX had remained around a level of 25 plus/minus 5 for most of the time in 2011, in August and again in September, we experienced a very strong increase in the index values—it reached nearly 50 at some stages.

While we are still far away from the levels of around 75 reached in October 2008, this development is certainly worrying. It reflects the high uncertainty induced by the recent worsening of the financial crisis.

It may seem odd to some observers to see exchange trading flourish in times when the rest of the economy is in deep trouble. However, just imagine how the financial markets would react to changes in market participants' expectations and worsening macroeconomic outlooks if exchange organizations did not exist. Would they refrain from restructuring their portfolios? Certainly not. But without exchange organizations, these restructurings would be taking place in risky, opaque and unreliable environments, in which frequent breakdowns of communication would be the rule rather than the exception. The absence of reference prices or of indices would vastly increase the insecurity of the markets. As a consequence, volatility would not be dampened—it would increase. And the resulting loss of confidence in the economy would be all the more severe.

To sum up: The globalization of exchange organizations is a natural response to increasing competition and to the globalization of the exchange organizations' major customers. Globalization is accompanied by a broadening of exchange services and products that enable the development of new risk management techniques. In sum, the globalization of exchange organizations makes markets, worldwide, more transparent, more reliable, and generally safer.

CHAPTER 4: COMPETITIVE CHALLENGES IN THE MARKETPLACE

Moderator: Joe Cangemi, *ConvergEx Group*
Bill Harts, *Thomson Reuters*
Alasdair Haynes*, *Chi-X Europe*
Peter Jenkins, *Ax Trading, LLC*
Rob Howe, *Liquidnet*
Gary Stone, *Bloomberg Tradebook LLC*
Wally Sullivan, *Pulse Trading*

JOE CANGEMI: Who benefits the most from today's markets, is it investors or broker dealers? I'll start with Gary Stone.

GARY STONE: Both groups benefit because today's competition has made the exchanges more responsive to their clients' needs. As a result, they are focusing more on different constituencies to create various models to satisfy each. The Philadelphia Stock Exchange is a good example of this. Philly is trying to use a combination of size, price, and time priorities for institutions that strive to trade in larger sizes.[1] Then there is the BATS's BZX Exchange pricing model that has resulted in reducing industry transaction

*Alasdair Haynes is founder and, as of writing, CEO of Aquis Exchange.

[1] NASDAQ subsequently scaled back this initiative in early 2013 at the Philadelphia Stock Exchange, formally known as NASDAQ OMX PSX, focusing instead on ETFs. The NASDAQ OMX PSX exchange was launched in September 2010 as Nasdaq's third stock-trading platform. "The ETF focus marks a retreat from NASDAQ's earlier plans for the exchange. The PSX is the only US stock exchange that offers a so-called price/size priority model, which was intended to lure market participants through the use of rebates. That model ranks its orders first on price and then on size. In the filing, the exchange operator says that model has been only marginally successful in garnering market share."
Source: Nasdaq Plans to Focus on EFTs With PSX Exchange. **Kaitlyn Kiernan, *The Wall Street Journal,* March 12, 2013. http://online.wsj.com/article/BT-CO-20130312-710196.html.**

R.A. Schwartz et al. (eds.), *The Economic Function of a Stock Exchange*, Zicklin School of Business Financial Markets Series, DOI 10.1007/978-3-319-10350-1_4

costs. That model has been adopted elsewhere if you consider the algorithms of broker dealers that are "takers."[2]

In fact, Elkins/McSherry data show that transaction costs overall have dropped about 25% since Reg NMS was enacted.[3] That is certainly a big drop. And it has occurred despite a lot of concerns about slicing and dicing of orders—that is, the entering of larger orders into the marketplace as a sequence of much smaller orders.

In general, high-frequency trading is a benefit to the marketplace. Spreads have narrowed since 2006 even during the high volatility periods in large-cap stocks where high-frequency traders are particularly active. Indeed, in 2008 a ban on short selling resulted in the high-frequency guys being out of the market. Several studies have since shown that with them out of the market, spreads actually widened dramatically and the depth of the NBBO collapsed.[4] High-frequency trading has certainly added a lot of liquidity to the market.

In the small- and mid-cap sector, I would argue that the results have been mixed, depending on volatility and spreads. Generally, if they are very volatile small- or mid-cap stocks, spreads have widened more than large caps. Everything, however, is not really rosy. We have a real market structure regulatory issue here for the Securities and Exchange Commission. There are a lot of conflicts in today's market structure which I will return to in a moment.

[2] Many other US exchanges have similar pricing models. Traders are either "makers" or "takers" of liquidity. Makers provide bids and offers, earning a rebate, their orders already are at the exchange; takers pay a fee, executing against those orders.

In November 2008, BATS converted its ECN to a national securities exchange, BZX, which allowed BATS to participate in and earn market data fees from the US consolidated tape plan, reduce its clearing costs and operate a primary listings business. In February 2010, BATS expanded into a new asset class by offering trading of listed equity options on BZX. In October 2010, BATS launched BYX, a second national securities exchange for trading listed cash equity securities. BATS launched a primary listings business in the US on its BZX Exchange in December 2010 and launched its first listings of seven ETFs in January 2012. With BYX, BATS offered a different pricing model than its larger market, BZX.

[3] Reg NMS (Regulation National Market System) was adopted by the Securities and Exchange Commission in 2005 and introduced 2 years later to further advance the ideals of a national market system. The regulation includes the order protection, or trade-through rule; access rule (fair access) to market data including quotations; rules on sub-penny trading and on market data.

[4] National Best Bid and Offer. SEC requirement that brokers must guarantee customers the best available ask and the best available bid prices when they buy and sell securities.

We talk a lot about high-frequency players. We talk a lot about what happened with the Flash Crash.[5] We put circuit breakers in place to deal with it. But that doesn't deal with another question: Who is protecting the integrity of the marketplace? Here is the problem: Exchanges are for-profit entities, a status which sets up a conflict between the business side and an exchange as a self-regulatory organization, or SRO. And regulation isn't clear on this. For-profit exchanges are dependent on high-frequency players not only for liquidity but also for transactions, co-location, data and other types of fees. The business side at the exchanges embraces paying customers of all forms regardless of their behavior and strategies. The exchange's self-regulatory body, on the other hand, is supposed to enforce the rules of the exchange. And, I would argue, the exchange's self-regulatory body is also there to protect the integrity of the marketplace. It is supposed to police bad behavior. Consequently, there is this natural conflict between the self-regulatory and the business sides. But it appears that the business side is winning.

An exchange in real time understands what is happening to its marketplace. For example, a member that is sending in 150,000 quotes in 10 ms—and then cancels them—appears to be just trying to slow the market down for some reason. But shouldn't the SRO kick that player out? Most people would say that's excessive quoting which doesn't contribute to liquidity, or to the price discovery process.

So why doesn't it happen? Profit is one motive. The business side fears such policing would drive participants to other competing exchanges.

Additionally, the SRO may feel that Reg NMS's Fair Access Rule, which requires the exchanges to provide fair access to market participants, restricts them from taking such a stand. The exchanges are not (and to some extent may feel that they cannot) protecting the integrity of their marketplace by shutting people off who are doing things to create latency issues or to engage in other bad behavior. Those are things we need to address. Perhaps the SEC should consider setting a principles-based rule that the exchange has the right or the obligation to police members in real-time that are compromising the fairness, operation and functioning of its marketplace?

PETER JENKINS: I agree with much of that. The markets have evolved further since Reg NMS. Transaction cost analysis is saying in general that costs are coming down for the institutional community. Nevertheless, I would assume that if you separate out the small-cap and micro-cap sector from the broader institutional marketplace, the costs for the micro-cap stocks

[5] Flash Crash, May 6, 2010. The Dow Jones Industrial Average sensationally declined about 1,000 points, or about 9% only to recover those losses within minutes.

have probably increased dramatically. I have seen some studies that support this. For the small-cap, tough to trade situations, the environment has become a bit more difficult. This is where alternative trading systems really play a role in the marketplace.

ALASDAIR HAYNES: I'll give you my perspective on the competition in the 15 markets in Europe where we compete. But first, my apologies if there is anybody in the audience who is Spanish. I am about to be rude about your country. I am sorry but one country has failed to comply with MiFID.[6] And that country is Spain! There are some interesting studies about this—one by professor Peter Gomber at Goethe University of Frankfurt. His study shows that the competition among the other 14 markets within the EU has resulted in narrower spreads, more liquidity, and reduced costs. So, in effect, this benefits every single investor, whether a broker dealer or an institution.

Yet there is one market, Spain, where prices[7] have actually risen, spreads have remained the same, and liquidity hasn't improved. Yes, we are talking about Spain. Spain is a great example of what happens when you don't have true competition in a market. Spain will be forced to change. Right now it is an excellent example of what happens when you don't change.[8]

CANGEMI: Bill, the line that differentiates an exchange and broker dealers has blurred. What has precipitated that? Where do you see that heading?

BILL HARTS: I listened to three friends of mine speak about it here earlier today: Gary Katz, Alfred Berkeley and Brett Redfearn. Each of them expressed it with a slightly different take on what's good and what's not good for the markets. That brings you back to the understanding that where you stand really depends on where you sit! [laughter]. Brokers have always thought about the competition from exchanges but, throughout history,

[6] Markets in Financial Instruments Directive, or MiFID, was officially enacted on November 1, 2007. The goal is to integrate the European Union's financial markets and to increase the amount of cross border investment orders.

[7] Referring to transactions and other costs.

[8] See, Global Regulatory Reform. The world of financial instruments just got more complex. Time to take note. Capital markets reform: MiFID II., Ernst & Young, http://www.ey.com/Publication/vwLUAssets/MiFID_II_adds_complexity_to_financial_instruments/$FILE/MiFID_II_adds_complexity_to_financial_instruments.pdf.
Financial Regulatory Reform: the Primary Driver Fueling Overhaul of Banking Operations. Ernst & Young LP, (PRWEB) January 14, 2013. http://www.prweb.com/releases/2013/1/prweb10315648.htm.

exchanges have been member-owned. There were always checks and balances in that competition. After exchanges demutualized, brokers became more concerned about it. One result of the concern that we see today is these various forms of internalization such as dark pools. I would like to touch on one area that illustrates where the competition is heading. It is something that several firms are working on—sponsored access.[9]

Let me tell you a story. Not so long ago I was approached by a large hedge fund client of the bank I worked for. The client wanted a direct connection to the exchange. We were concerned about it for reasons I will explain. On the other hand, we wanted to appear to accommodate such a large client who really wanted direct connectivity. So we approached our lawyer, and the conversation went something like, "Listen this client really wants to do this. Can we do it? Well, actually, please tell us that we can't do it!" Of course, a good lawyer will always tell you that you can't do something. So we went back to the client and said, "Listen we would really like to give you this direct access to the exchange but our lawyer tells us that we just can't let you do it."

What were we worried about? First, all of these things are still true today as they were back then. To begin with, there was the inability of our trading desk to interact with the customer's order flow. That is, when flow goes directly to an exchange, the broker essentially loses the ability to interact with it. The second one was to protect ourselves, our bank and our client from things like fat finger risk and systematic errors.[10] As someone pointed out earlier, just because you can do something doesn't mean you automatically should do it, or that it is even in your best interest. Third, we were worried about the competition from exchanges. Fourth, we really worried that, with a flip of the switch, we could be completely removed from the client relationship. We were worried about being completely disintermediated.[11]

[9] The practice by a bank or brokerage of facilitating direct market access for a client to an exchange without any pre-trade risk management. In this way, for example, a high-frequency trading firm would have access to low-latency markets without pre-execution controls. Sponsored access has many different meanings and nuances for market participants. Its origin can be traced back to the practice of direct market access (DMA), a practice in which a broker member of an exchange provides its market participant identification (MPID) and exchange connectivity infrastructure to a customer in order to send trades directly to the exchange.

[10] Fat finger risk is the risk of clumsy human errors in the trading process caused by misplaced keystrokes and the like. Systematic errors are associated with erroneous data entry.

[11] For example, the client might have an order to buy 50,000 shares of ZYZ via this sponsored access arrangement directly at the NYSE. At the same time, the broker sponsoring this sponsored access might have been willing to sell the client 50,000 shares of ZYZ had it

Today the SEC has basically chosen to remove some of these barriers, and to replace them with some others. I'll leave it up to Steve Wunsch[12] to figure out the unintended consequences. It will become an important front in the competition between exchanges and brokers.

CANGEMI: Rob, does exchange consolidation address the needs of institutions? What does it all mean?

ROB HOWE: The short answer is no. At Liquidnet we have a unique perspective on the exchange space based on our customer community. This community comprises the largest asset managers in the world. Consolidation doesn't really address the needs of these institutions, nor of our customer base. If you look at this historically, exchanges have not adequately addressed the needs of the buy-side institutions. We heard earlier about what exchanges are focused on these days—data products, derivatives, even catering to high-frequency traders. The constituents that are left out are the large, long-only asset managers. At Liquidnet, we are working with the exchanges aiming to address those needs. One example is a recent announcement we made with the Swiss Stock Exchange that allows its customers to send large blocks safely into Liquidnet's liquidity pool.[13] This helps both the Swiss Exchange customers and the Liquidnet customers. It really combines the best of both our worlds—the wholesale marketplace of Liquidnet, and the retail market place of an exchange. It also helps with exchanges going global. We will allow these Swiss stock exchanges to trade in five additional markets: Switzerland, Germany, France, the UK and Netherlands [14] We feel that it could also benefit the country as a whole. As efficiency comes to the capital formation process, more investment dollars can flow into the country.

CANGEMI: Peter, how is the domination of high-frequency trading on exchanges affecting the institutional investor? Do high-frequency trading, HFT shops, as "the new market makers," constantly posting bids and offers, satisfy the needs of those institutional traders?

known about the order but yet would have been effectively "disintermediated" because of the arrangement.

[12] Steve Wunsch is a well-recognized industry expert on market structure and the former CEO and pioneer of the now defunct electronic Arizona Stock Exchange (AZX).

[13] Press Release: SIX Swiss Exchange and Liquidnet Launch New Block Equities Trading Service. SIX Swiss Exchange first to deliver global institutional liquidity to its members through unique trading model. Liquidnet brings previously untapped block liquidity from five European markets to its global institutional trading network. (Business Wire, July 08, 2011) See http://www.businesswire.com/news/home/20110708005161/en/Swiss-Exchange-Liquidnet-Launch-Block-Equities-Trading.

[14] The service was expanded in 2012 and now includes Belgian, Danish, Finnish, Austrian, Portuguese and Swedish equities.

JENKINS: As I said before, some stocks, or classes of stocks, trade differently than others. Since Reg NMS, the high-frequency community has developed a lot of liquidity in a small group of stocks. I am not too sure that just because the spread in a stock has tightened, this necessarily means that this is the right price and that share prices are not bouncing around too much. But I do think that high-frequency traders have added liquidity, that they have become the market makers in the new environment, and that the old NYSE specialist is now more of an electronic market maker.[15] Has it helped the small-cap stocks, the micro-cap stocks, or a very large situational customer? No. I think that flow is increasingly avoiding exchanges and going to the broker dealer in an effort to find the natural other side.

There are some situations where I go back to my buy-side days in my approach. In these situations, in other words, one would rather deal with a natural counterparty in the trading of some stocks. One does not necessarily need a market marker putting up capital even in the smallest amount. I agree that, in part of the marketplace, things do look good, and costs have come down. But there are other areas of the marketplace that need help, that need more development. If the ATS environment fills that void, that is fine by me.

CANGEMI: Back in my days on the New York Stock Exchange floor, the biggest complaint from most of my customers was finding liquidity in small-cap and mid-cap stocks. Some of you in the room today no doubt remember some of those conversations. It was challenging for market makers to publicly display what they wanted to buy and sell in a stock that didn't trade very frequently. I agree with you, Peter. In a lot of ways, we are still searching for solutions to problems that have always existed. And thank you again Bob for putting a great conference like this together so we can get people to air these important topics publicly.

Alasdair, without specifically talking about high-frequency trading, could you tell us what size and speed mean to the markets today? How do they affect trading?

HAYNES: Size and speed are important but not in the way that most people think. There was an interesting discussion in the early panel about speed. Is there a race? Every exchange is competing to become faster, faster and more faster! Alfred Berkeley mentioned earlier about blinking. We all

[15] "The cornerstone of the NYSE market model is the Designated Market Maker or DMM. Formerly known as "Specialists," DMMs are the only participant to have true obligations for maintaining fair and orderly markets for their assigned securities. They operate both manually and electronically to facilitate price discovery during market openings, closings, and during periods of substantial trading imbalances or instability. This "high-touch" approach is crucial for improving prices, dampening volatility, adding liquidity and enhancing value." Source: NYSE.

have to blink. I bet you don't know this amazing fact: the dung-loving fungus is actually the fastest thing in nature on this planet! Not many people have heard of the dung-loving fungus, and of the spores that are omitted from it. You may know that the sparrow hawk is the fastest bird; it reaches terminal velocity when it is actually catching its prey. Do you know that the cheetah is the fastest mammal?

Actually, comparative speeds at this level are irrelevant when it comes down to the nanoseconds, picoseconds, zeptoseconds, and femtoseconds. Look at the human species: we sit on the top of the food chain and we are pretty slow. I am looking at some of you around here! (laughter). I am pretty slow. But the truth is, we are well configured. That is what an exchange is about when it comes to speed. It's not about how fast you can move. It's how well configured you are to receive all the information.

People talk about information, about the number of quotes and the number of fills versus quotes. It is ridiculous in the long term to think that regulators will try to police that because it is impossible. It is great rhetoric, it wins votes with politicians, but it is just impractical. What you need are exchanges that have capacity. Technology is here. And Moore's law illustrates that.[16]

We will get faster, and quicker, and more efficient. Chi-X Europe is the largest exchange in Europe by volume, and by value traded. And we are not even the fastest exchange. However, we are about to become the fastest exchange and, sure enough, in 9 months' time someone else is likely to become even faster because of the industry dynamics.[17] Yes, it is just going to leap frog us! Still, as long as we are in that fast zone we can compete.

Speed is one thing. The other is size. Size is important not because you have to be big. Remember the dinosaurs? They were pretty big but they didn't last. Size is important because you actually need to be small. You need to be efficient. You need to be effective. The reason we can eat the lunch of the national exchanges is because we are just so much smaller. Chi-X Europe has a staff of 47. That is actually slightly less than the catering departments of all the national exchanges in Europe. In other words, as an electronic market like Chi-X, you need to be as cost-effective as possible. That means being scalable enough to quickly grow your trading

[16] "The number of transistors incorporated in a chip will approximately double every 24 months," according to Gordon Moore, Intel co-founder.

[17] The project to turn Chi-X into the "fastest exchange" as described in the speaker's comment was ultimately discontinued, according to a spokesperson for Haynes in a follow-up after this conference.

volume with minimum overhead costs as you expand. In short, you leverage the economies of scale.

HARTS: A lot of people have talked about how markets are more efficient because of electronic trading. To some extent they actually are if you look carefully at spreads and other measures like that. A number of studies tell us so. But it's important to remember that all of this electronic trading has also saddled us collectively, as an industry, with hundreds of millions of dollars, if not billions of dollars, of infrastructure costs that we continue to spend year after year in order to cope with the increasing number of quotes, communications lines, servers, and other requirements. This tends to get lost sometimes when people think about the efficiency of markets.

STONE: Fairness is also called for in terms of infrastructure. Everyone perceives market data in an equal light. Your ability to buy your way into closer proximity to the matching engine shouldn't necessarily give you an unfair advantage.

HAYNES: We would agree. The quality of an exchange is extremely important. However it is all well and good when all men are created equal and some are more equal than others! You also have to think that latency is important to only a handful of people when you are dealing with microseconds. It is a random walk world, and most people don't necessarily have to be the first ones there. You have to weigh the pros and cons. The average retail investor doesn't care if he or she is trading in microseconds. There is this lovely idea about uninformed flow. The uniformed flow that I have found historically has been pretty well informed. I don't think you necessarily have to build an exchange which allows 500 different members of it to be co-located, or to have proximity solutions that are equal. But you do have to allow equal access to those who want it. That's the important part and that is where you get equality.

CANGEMI: Wally, let's talk about the Trade-At Rule from the SEC's Concept Release of 2010.[18] I will give a brief description of what Trade-At offered for discussion. Trade-At requires all non-transparent markets to utilize the National Best Bid or Offer, NBBO, of the transparent markets to price transactions 'off exchange' with minimum price improvement required.

Wally, a majority of the industry responses were not in favor of implementing it. The concept continues to surface in the press and, among the regulators, it seems to come up in every other sentence. What are your thoughts on the impact on exchange structure if the SEC actually were to file a new rule on this?

[18] See, Thoughts on Trade-At Rule, Themis Trading. April 19, 2010. (http://blog.themistrading.com/thoughts-on-trade-at-rule/.

SULLIVAN: If the Trade-At Rule was implemented it would negatively impact internalization models and drive some of that flow back towards traditional exchanges. I personally think this rule will never be implemented because of the significant decrease in overall equity volumes it would cause. The rule appears to target internalization models, populated by high-frequency trading, or HFT, by requiring price improvement. Even a half cent price improvement would ruin the risk reward model that HFT players operate. Without the liquidity that these HFT firms provide, internalization cross rates would plummet. I would not want to be the regulator that pushes through this rule change only to see equity volumes cut in half the next day.

Concern about high-frequency participants is understandable. But the reality is they currently play an important role as the new industry market makers. My issue is that they have become so dominant they have squeezed out most participants that had a fiduciary responsibility to make markets. This sets the stage for some unstable market swings if these high-frequency trading participants decide not to show up. They don't have any fiduciary responsibility to make markets. They can step away anytime they want. They were able to garner the majority of daily equity volumes by responding with faster technology to the institutional trend of using Direct Market Access, or DMA algos, that cut larger orders into 100-share orders or print sizes. Print size is important because their models don't work with larger orders The HFT guys will all tell you that they can't make money trading amongst themselves. They only survive off the retail flow and the sliced up institutional flow that we send them.

We at Pulse operate a system that is not an internalization model. It uses blotter integration, meaning we aggregate order flow from the blotters[19]—the electronic platforms where all of the original institutional orders reside, so it is further upstream. It reads these buy-side blotters. Like a Liquidnet, it matches natural block liquidity further upstream before it reaches an exchange. The appropriate and intelligent response to the high-frequency participants is to improve the efficiency of this upstream technology to match more of the natural liquidity. It is happening. In fact, there are some things happening behind the scenes among electronic trading platforms that basically improves block crossing efficiency.[20]

[19] For example, when a portfolio manager makes a decision to say buy 300,000 shares of IBM the order gets loaded onto firm's buyside "blotter." Orders then get disseminated into the market from the blotter.

[20] Sullivan was referring to platforms such as Liquidnet that added innovative services to improve block crossing rates.

Blotter integration technologies are just casting a much wider net. The other thing to note is that some of the dark pools—and there is only a handful of them in this county—trade blocks 5,000 shares and above.[21] A lot of these use blotter integration technology.

As electronic communications in the industry continue to improves, this technology will help to solve the ships passing in the night problem.[22] Right now, if you look at how much chunky, block liquidity is associated with these algos, it is staggering. It is billions of shares of actual block liquidity a day.

The industry is healing itself. It is using innovative techniques that will counterbalance the high-frequency guys. Every 10,000 share block print translates into 20,000 shares, counting both sides of the trade, that don't feed the high-frequency guys. Instead of 60–70% of the marketplace being dominated by high-frequency guys, I wouldn't be surprised if shortly down the road that drops to 40% or 50%.[23] In this scenario, you would eventually see the institutional volumes trading in higher print sizes, and perhaps bringing more influence in the marketplace.

CANGEMI: So you are predicting bigger block prints in a greater percentage of the tape somewhere down the road? There are a lot of customers thanking you very much right now![24]

SULLIVAN: I wouldn't necessarily say we'll see large block trading make a huge comeback. What you will see, I think, is a resurgence of

[21] ITG, Liquidnet and BlockCross.

[22] Ships passing in the night is a popular trading metaphor describing block trading opportunities missed because of a market structure that can result in both sides of a block cross missing each other like ships passing on the ocean in the dark of night. In the world of electronic trading today, this has a particular resonance.
"In many instances, for a dark pool trade to take place, a buyer has to be present before a seller can initiate a sale. This is called iceberg trading. The "iceberg" being the buyer. Sometimes, however, a seller doesn't emerge to consummate the transaction at the same time a buyer is floating by. This is called 'ships passing in the night,'" notes Jeremy Butler, author of Dark Pools Rising, Trading in the Dark, Valueline, April 25, 2013.

[23] "HFT [high-frequency trading] accounts for about 50–70% of US trades, 40% in Canada, 35% in London and about 15–20% of ASX [Australia Stock Exchange] equities trading," according to a business article in Business Insider Australia that cited a study. See, STUDY: High Frequency Trading Makes Markets More Fair, Business Insider Australia, Liz Tay, December 09, 2013, **http://www.businessinsider.com.au/high-frequency-trading-makes-markets-more-fair-by-mitigating-the-effects-of-manipulation-researchers-say-2013-12.**

[24] On November 07, 2013, the New York Stock Exchange proposed "A One Year Pilot Program That Would Add New Rule 107D To Establish An Institutional Liquidity Program." See, http://www.nyse.com/nysenotices/nyse/rule-filings/pdf;jsessionid=07B5DBBA5CC5AB310C99B1FE9DC0B4F3?file_no=SR-NYSE-2013-72&seqnum=1.

medium-size prints. There are stats that show that high-frequency guys can't play when you start dealing in print sizes above 700 shares. If the institutional community improves the efficiency of matching up natural liquidity, that will act as a natural counterbalance. Because you will have stopped the high-frequency guys. It should be noted that if the industry continues its current trend toward passive investing techniques, then much of the impact of improved block trading efficiencies will be diminished. Indexing and the use of ETFs have greatly reduced the number of institutional orders available for crossing.[25]

HARTS: Let's be clear. Trade-At, if implemented, would result in much more volume being printed and executed on exchanges. All the different forms of internalization will suffer if it is implemented. Yet from an exchange's standpoint you really have to be sympathetic. They don't want to be the liquidity pool of last resort. They want to be the liquidity pool you go to first. A lot of the upstream marketplaces or market centers effectively circumvent that. That is what the talk about Trade-At is really describing.[26]

CANGEMI: Trade-At is a concept that will drive flow to the floors or to the exchange centers for printing. Because if all markets must price improve off the NBBO at economically adverse levels, the alternative markets could not compete. I wonder though whether regulation will try to obliterate any solutions put in place, the ones being talked about, and being built to satisfy investors today, especially institutional investors. Transparency or opaque strategies for investors have always been an integral part of the investment process. I am not here to preach a sermon, although that is what I have done for 25 years!

It is something that academics really need to weigh in on very arduously, if Trade-At does emerge.[27] I believe it will. I think there is another discussion

[25] In a subsequent interview for this book in October 2013, Sullivan explained that this trend had accelerated in the wake of the conference. "It was starting to take hold and already happening back then at the time of the conference," Sullivan said. "But nobody had really recognized it at that time."

[26] By the spring of 2013, exchange executives, worried about the volume of trading moving off exchanges and onto platforms like dark pools, were pushing for enactment of a "Trade-At" rule, which would allow a trade to occur away from an exchange only if the customer was getting a significantly better price than was available on an exchange.

[27] "I wouldn't say it is dead but it was a long shot from the beginning as was noted earlier in this discussion," commented Joe Cangemi, the moderator, in a follow-up in October 2013 for this chapter, referring to the Trade-At Rule. "The exchanges have been trying to force the SEC and Congress to get involved and mandate such a rule but the resistance is high based on the arguments. No one has proven that the client is adversely impacted by the competitive model currently in place."

coming because the proposal just doesn't want to go away. I am in Washington twice a month, and it comes up there every time.[28] It doesn't want to come up in our industry, but it does come up in Washington. So I give everyone pause, and I give everyone caution on that subject.

Peter, have institutional brokers become more or less aligned with exchanges?

JENKINS: I would say that they have become more aligned with the exchanges in a certain portion of their volume. Algorithmic flow is a much larger portion of their business than ever before. But then again, this has not changed over the years, especially with internalization and the efforts by institutional brokers to match up customers' orders. Satisfying their best execution obligations at times forces brokers to match up customers orders if they do not immediately think it is the right thing to go to an exchange.[29] This is especially the case today in an environment where high-frequency trading volume dominates. So these brokers are aligned with the exchanges because they are doing more volume algorithmically today than ever before. But there is that portion of their business where they are trying to cross it upstairs and to satisfy their best execution obligation for the institution.[30]

STONE: We have been very equity focused. The options exchanges actually have done a good job of attracting the institutional investors. The best example would probably be the spread books.[31] A lot of institutional investors don't want leg risks in their different spreads.[32] If you are doing a volatility trade, you have to do a stock with an option.

[28] Joe (Joseph) Cangemi was Chairman of the Security Traders Association, January 2011–December 2011. He was visiting Washington in his capacity as an industry leader and professional.

[29] Reg NMS, adopted by the Securities and Exchange Commission in 2005, laid out guidelines on "best execution" and order protection to thwart the execution of trades at prices that are lower than the protected quotations displayed on other markets.

[30] Upstairs trading, or off exchange trading, today includes the panoply of off-exchange platforms such as ATSs and dark pools.

[31] Spread books and complex order books are regarded as the same thing depending on the exchange. For a more detailed explanation, See, ISE Options Exchange document, http://www.ise.com/assets/files/market_data/Spreads_Feed/ISE_Spreads_Book_Feed_Specification.pdf.

See, also, CBOE on Complex Order Books, http://www.cboe.com/COB/COB.aspx.

[32] In a subsequent explanation for this chapter, the speaker explained that, "if you get legged, you still need to complete the other side or you are not hedged. When you complete it, you may have slippage—that's the difference between the intended spread and where you got done." The speaker offered this example. A spread of 10: buy at 10, sell at 20. Let's say you get lifted at 20. And you go to hit the bid, but the market goes 10 offer. If you sell at 9, your

The options exchanges have done a very good job of creating spread books as a package. If you don't have leg risk, it either happens or it doesn't. And there are certain instances where it has occurred. As exchanges consolidate you may also see more consolidation of different asset classes. That triggers the innovation we are looking for.

CANGEMI: So consolidation is a benefit in that sense?

STONE: Yes, to some extent.

CANGEMI: Risk is a big part of what makes our markets competitive. I don't like to take risk out of it.

STONE: It depends on what the risk is.[33]

CANGEMI: Rob, what must exchanges do to remain viable today?

HOWE: I can only comment from an equity perspective. I think we saw it with the Deutsche Börse presentation today that equity trading is a smaller part of the exchanges revenue base now. For both the NYSE and NASDAQ, equity trading is now less than 20% of their revenue. They are focused on other products. To remain viable, it goes back to a point I made earlier. Exchanges really need to focus on their core customer base on the equity side. That is publicly-traded corporations, as well as the buy-side trading institutions. Exchanges need to innovate, they need to bring in new products and services, and they have to be global.

HAYNES: You are absolutely right. What is important for an exchange is to build market share. This is a very contentious issue in Europe. The cost of market data in the US is seven to nine times less than in Europe. Clearing is seven to ten times cheaper here than in Europe. But if you look at the profits being made by exchanges from data and clearing alone—they are huge. London makes about £193 million a year from data services. Euronext makes some 200 million Euros a year. At Deutsche Börse, it is about 190 million Euros and, at NASDAQ, it is about $70 million. These are not small numbers. In Europe, this adds up to an 800 million Euros data services business. In contrast, it is between seven, nine, or ten times more expensive than in the US. Competition can drive that cost down, and that is exactly what has to happen.

spread isn't 10 but 11, so you have "slippage" of 1. See, Legging Risk definition, Automated Trader.
http://www.automatedtrader.net/glossary/Legging+risk

33 Stone explained in a follow-up interview that he was talking in broad terms about the risks associated mostly with market systems such as circuit breakers that are triggered when trading occurs within certain parameters. That in turn helps to reduce systemic risk.

What worried me with Reto Francioni's[34] speech at this conference today was his talk about Deutsche Börse going to a vertical business model. Of course, I could do every product if I had a monopoly. But does the world really want to see a monopoly? We want to see monopolies broken to stimulate competition. You don't get competition in vertical silos.

HARTS: If exchanges really want to be successful, they must focus on their biggest customers, rather than focusing on the high-frequency, low-latency players looking to arbitrage market data fees, exchange fees, capture rebates, and so on. While activity of that kind appears to pump up market volume, it doesn't do much to help its biggest customers.

HAYNES: There are four things that an exchange must do to survive. First, they need a strategy that has a clear goal for growth. If you don't have that you will not succeed. I worry that some exchanges around the world take their business for granted. They have no strategy for growth, and no sensible business plan. You have to build market share. You can have the most innovative, creative, brilliant system, but if you don't build market share you will not survive. If you don't do this, you can't sell data; and you can't provide the other products around it. You need sustainability. That is one of the things that we did at Chi-X, and we became profitable about 2 years ago. When I started at Chi-X, I was told, "Oh, don't worry about these guys, they are all going to go bust, they are never going to make money, they are never going to be around." Well, once you become profitable, as we did, you are sustainable, you can grow the business. And that is key.

The final point is one that most people laugh at me for. That is social responsibility, or social utility. There is a reason for an exchange to be here. There is a social reason to drive prices down for the greater good. You can never forget that we don't list stocks at Chi-X Europe, but if we grow the depth of liquidity in a marketplace, we will lower the cost of capital. And this is a big objective that exchanges are here to accomplish—to facilitate the issuance of new shares. If a company lowers its cost of capital by issuing shares, than we have done something for the greater good of the economy. That is what competition accomplishes. Those things are essential in any strategy for an exchange.

CANGEMI: The debate about market data and the costs of processing that data is on the verge of attracting major attention. The exchanges have been monetizing the data they control by selling it back to the very same investors who are creating it. The market structure is forcing those in the industry to buy the fastest and deepest data pools available to remain

[34] Reto Francioni, CEO, Deutsche Börse AG.

competitive—and these costs are growing exponentially. The markets are an eco-system and they require all to make contributions to its survival. The economics as they exist today were becoming unbalanced. Some of the discussions I have had in Washington lead me to believe, from a consolidated standpoint, that anyone sitting up here, or anyone servicing any customer need, must process market data in an efficient and effective manner.[35] Where or how they get that market data, whether it should be regulated or priced, can certainly be debated. It is a big part of exchange survival.

Let's look now into our crystal ball. What does the exchange space look like in 2020? Alasdair, will you start off?

HAYNES: I couldn't begin to tell you how it is going to look in a couple of weeks. In 2020? That is an impossible question to answer! But projecting 9 years into 2020, whether I am right or wrong, you won't be able to track me down! That aside, I actually think it is not that hard to look at what exchanges will be like because of consolidation. They will be more global.

One of the reasons, in fact, for the success of Chi-X in Europe is this: asset managers view Europe as one economic region and make their decision to invest based on Europe as a region. However, when they come to trade shares, Europe is divided into 30-odd national exchanges in terms of their stock listings, rules and other factors. There has never been a pan-European market, a single regional exchange—until now. So we at Chi-X have given the industry, predominantly the sell-side, a marketplace where trading reflects the way the investment decision is made—and this has been very popular. We are a new exchange where you can trade shares across Europe—UK, French and Swiss stocks, for example—all in one place. In effect, we are a "super-market" rather than a series of separate UK, French and Swiss grocery shops. There is no doubt in my mind that, just as the Internet has changed the way people shop from being local to global, equity trading is moving from being local to being global. Exactly what period of time will all this occur? I don't

[35] The moderator was visiting Washington and speaking as an industry leader and on a professional basis. Cangemi explained in a follow-up how the exchanges are required to provide data to the so-called Securities Industry Processor, or SIP. SIP in turn consolidates and disseminates all prices for the industry. The cost of the consolidated data is reasonable, he contended, and the proceeds of those sales are redistributed back to the exchanges equal to the ratio of their contribution to it.

"The problem is that using the consolidated data from an institutional perspective is not effective because of the latency experienced when compared to the speed of the data you can buy from the exchanges directly and consolidate yourself," Cangemi added. "The cost of which is what we are hostage to—and is unregulated by the SEC. The exchanges are not incented to provide a better consolidated product as that would adversely impact the sale of their other non-regulated data packages they sell directly."

know. Yes, maybe by 2020 we will see this. Events are moving in that direction.

The other thing is this: The four or five players who survive will be of two types. The analogy here is the airline industry. On the one hand, it is exactly the same as the national incumbent airlines that have now merged or joined together in alliances like Star Alliance or One World. They serve a certain purpose and serve an important sector of the market. On the other hand, you will have people in our industry who operate the low-budget airline model that serve another important sector of the market. The late Lord King, as CEO at British Airways, assumed the business community would always want to sit in a comfortable lounge and always travel on British Airways. He made a mistake. The important thing is that you want to travel safely, and the fastest and cheapest way possible.

This analogy is good to recall when you board an airplane, whether it is Jet Blue, American Airlines, RyanAir, EasyJet, or whomever. You are assured that the civil aviation authority makes certain the plane is safe. In exactly the same way, we need regulation that makes it absolutely safe for every platform that you trade on. In this regard, regulation is key. So you will end up with just two types of trading platforms. The economics is simply that you can't have 50 players trying to play in this game. Price pressure will allow only four or five people to survive. There will be a war of attrition and different styles of business. And the game has just begun.

CANGEMI: Anyone else want to take a stab at that?

HARTS: If history has shown us one thing, it's that exchange consolidation and fragmentation are cyclical. It turns around every 5 to 7 years. What Alasdair just said is absolutely true. However, following that consolidation you will see yet another round of fragmentation. The short answer is that, in 2020, I think we will likely look exactly as we do today (Laughter).

STONE: I will say clearing. Whatever happens in the clearing space will drive the exchange space. Just imagine a world right now where we have Dodd-Frank,[36] and fragmented swap execution facilities. They will all be competing, and you can choose the clearing counterparty of your choice. Imagine what happens to the futures market if Dodd-Frank goes into this market so you can actually clear anything you want into the CME's clearing

[36] Dodd-Frank Wall Street Reform and Consumer Protection Act, known as Dodd-Frank, was signed into law by President Barack Obama on July 21, 2010. The sweeping consumer protection and regulatory reform law also includes the controversial Volcker Rule that prohibits proprietary trading by depository banks. The rule was passed by regulators on December 10, 2013. See, Financial regulators approve long-awaited Volcker Rule. James O'Toole, CNNMoney. http://money.cnn.com/2013/12/10/news/economy/volcker-rule/index.html.

house.[37] That would fragment and take away transactions from the clearing space that could disrupt the entire exchange system. If we are going global, you need the ability to take the stock that you traded 24 h ago in Germany and bring it back to the states in a cost-efficient way, because that is where your custodial bank is located. If that occurs, you will have amazing competition within the exchange space. But it is being driven by what's going on in the clearing side.

HOWE: In the future, we will see efficiencies on two fronts around trading. One is ideas. We will see that the best investment is not necessarily what's in your backyard anymore. It is going to be the US portfolio manager looking for that health care stock in Thailand or Indonesia. We will see a flow of investment ideas around the world. The second is around trading and efficiency. We will continue to see the barriers to trading coming down. We will see that liquidity will seamlessly flow around the globe, and that trading will be more efficient because there will be two marketplaces. There will be a wholesale marketplace for size, and there will be a retail market place for the smaller executions that we see on the exchanges.

JENKINS: The one thing that doesn't change is the continuing role for a dealer using its capital. But we will swing from bigger use of dealer capital to getting more efficiency by matching up natural buyers and sellers. Technology has made it more efficient for large players to trade with each other. But if the numbers are right, and if the high-frequency proprietary traders are 50–60% or so of the volume, the buy-side institutions are probably starting to use more broker capital on block trades as brokers dealers are more comfortable with this new structure—and are willing to take a little more risk for their institutional traders upstairs. Because they understand how they can hedge or get out of these positions. That is my observation. Proprietary capital is being used to match buyers and sellers. So there will be a trend back to people who will think up ways to get the natural buyers and sellers together.

CANGEMI: Questions from the audience?

JOE ROSEN [RKA Inc.]: Some would suggest that if you want to talk about a level playing field from a regulatory perspective, then all manner of ATSs in the US should be regulated the same way as exchanges.

HAYNES: I will just jump in from Europe to clear this one! We hear constantly that we have this inadequate regulation in our exchange. This is completely and utterly untrue. I say that without getting into the technical

[37] As Stone noted in a follow-up interview, the implications of this change would be extraordinary. Today, for example, a 10-year note future can only clear via the CME. Under this scenario, if this could then be cleared through the ICS clearing facilities, the implications would be far-reaching.

details of MiFID and the various parts of regulation.[38] We have 4,000 pages of regulation to comply with as an MTF.[39] The exchanges have only about 150 pages of regulation. If you just do it on the sheer weight of paper, we clearly have more regulation to comply with. We have written to the European Union asking, will you please standardize this regulation and take this argument away once and for all? If people think we are easily regulated, then people don't travel on our plane.

CANGEMI: It is a challenging question. The exchanges have all created broker dealers to, in effect, compete in the broker dealer space as well. It is an evolving regulatory question that probably will have clarity by 2020. I am not sure if we will have the right answer by then, but perhaps there will be some more clarity.

THOMSON REUTERS [Reporter]: Most people would say that, as far as high-frequency trading is concerned, the chief opportunity is in exploiting market inefficiency. But if you talk to a lot of prop traders, if you talk to a lot of high-frequency traders, you will find that right now that space is becoming much more competitive. There is a lot less opportunity to exploit market inefficiency there today. Do you think that, in the near term, the problem will work itself out? Or, do you think that there is something that needs to be done collaboratively across the exchanges to help increase market efficiency?

CANGEMI: Are you asking whether we are going to regulate how and where high-frequency trading can make money? I was only kidding. It sounded that way though. It is certainly taking the opposite approach.

THOMSON REUTERS: In all seriousness, talk to a bunch of prop traders and high-frequency traders about those opportunities. I don't want to say that there are fewer opportunities. But as more competition enters that space, those opportunities become more difficult for individual firms to take advantage of. So, then the question is, do you think that this is a problem? Or is there a critical mass that we hit and the problem just solves itself? Or are the challenges around algorithmic trading?

CANGEMI: Here's my take. Short-term trading capital has always existed in the marketplace, it always will. It will find a vehicle to put itself to work. When you look at the players here, and at some people in the audience, the various ways you can trade today are almost limitless. They are global, in the sense that you can execute your trades in both the domestic US

[38] Markets in Financial Instruments Directive, or MiFID, was officially enacted on November 1, 2007. The goal is to integrate the European Union's financial markets and to increase the amount of cross border investment orders.

[39] MTF, or multilateral trading facility, originally identified in MiFID, are pan-European electronic trading platforms unique to Europe.

market and in numerous non-US markets across the globe. A lot of the high-frequency trading in the US prior to 2008 and 2009 is now being done internationally. Whether it is on the Canadian exchange or on some of the European exchanges. The short-term money that was conceptually housed in the US market has moved abroad to take advantage of better margins in other trading regions. High-frequency trading does not use investment capital per-se. It is funded by what is called "short-term" money, which can be defined as capital which is to be invested for the shortest possible period of time allowing for limited risk but adequate return. I don't think it is ever going away. Do you agree?

JENKINS: Yes, I agree. There will be a movement of liquidity to less efficient markets because of trading participants and dealers being opportunistic as markets outside the US continue to work out the kinks in the early modernizing stages of their own, evolving electronic market structures. The dealers look to where the opportunities are. But that is a temporary phenomenon. Because ultimately those kinds of cost advantages are short lived and get arbitraged away as these less efficient markets complete their changes. The capital and money will then flow back to the US markets. I fear that trying to regulate it can cause problems. If we put in a Trade-At Rule that might even increase that amount of high-frequency trading, forcing volume to a specific venue. I am against the idea of trying to regulate that out. We need intermediaries to step in when there is no other side to the trade.

HAYNES: I might be slightly semantic. You talked about high-frequency traders exploiting market inefficiencies. I would turn that slightly on its head and say, I believe that high-frequency trading is trying to create better market efficiency. You look at the reason why speed and price are so related—it is because of the risk you take. I am thinking of European stocks right now. If I asked you to make a price in 10 million shares, and you held the price for an hour, your price would be a mile wide in terms of the spread. If I asked you to do it in a minute it will be a lot tighter. If I asked you to do it for a second it is going to be even tighter. The smaller you go, the faster you go, the more risk you are willing to take in size. Most people think that high-frequency trading is all about trying to exploit inefficiencies. I see it as a method of creating a better use of capital in the marketplace. By no means are they all angels. There is a real role to be played by these high-frequency players, and there is a strong correlation between speed and the amount of risk.

CANGEMI: Thank you all very much.

CHAPTER 5: WHEREIN LIE THE GROWTH OPPORTUNITIES?

Moderator: Bruce Weber, *Lerner College of Business and Economics, University of Delaware*
Ian Domowitz, *ITG*
Pinar Emirdag, *London Stock Exchange*
Frank Hatheway, *NASDAQ OMX*
Tim Mahoney, *BIDS Trading*
Joe Rosen, *RKA Inc.*
Larry Tabb, *TABB Group*

ROBERT SCHWARTZ: I look forward to welcoming our panels and moderators. This next panel is no exception, and it is really very special. As many of you well know, Bruce Weber and I go back a long way. We have collaborated on numerous projects, including our TraderEx[1] software simulation product.

I first met Bruce in 1990 when he was pursuing post-doctoral research in London. We were later together as academicians at NYU. We were together again as faculty at Baruch College. Bruce was the founding director of Baruch's Subotnick Financial Services Center. Then Bruce transferred across the Atlantic to the London Business School. And now he is back in the US. Today, Bruce is a Dean. Not just an Assistant Dean, not an Associate Dean. Yes, Bruce is the Dean at the Lerner College of Business and Economics, University of Delaware. We've royalty on our hands. It is a great pleasure to welcome Bruce.

BRUCE WEBER: I don't know if I will allow you to take the podium Bob before I get started the next time! (laughter).

Wherein lie the growth opportunities? Stock exchange share prices have kind of looked like those nice picture of Mount Fuji in travel books. You had this great run up in their prices right after demutualization 10 to 15 years ago, and then this gorgeous peak at the end of 2007. Since then stock exchange revenue has been flat, the returns to investors have been unimpressive and mostly negative—and that's the steep slide, the backside of the mountain. It seems as if exchanges are really struggling to grow in the current

[1] See, TraderEx website for more details, http://www.etraderex.com/.

R.A. Schwartz et al. (eds.), *The Economic Function of a Stock Exchange*, Zicklin School of Business Financial Markets Series, DOI 10.1007/978-3-319-10350-1_5

environment. Is that because of the industry's competitive, yet regulated structure? Is it something about the way the technology and the trading industry have evolved?

Maybe it is difficult for the traditional exchanges to do well because of how the securities markets have evolved. We heard Alasdair Haynes this morning note that Chi-X Europe[2] operates with just 47 employees, yet it is one of the largest venues in Europe. So you have some disruptive competitors[3] in this industry. What are the traditional exchanges, such as the London Stock Exchange, the New York Stock Exchange and NASDAQ, supposed to do? Where will they find growth opportunities? Let's ask the panel. I'll start with Larry.

LARRY TABB: The issues for exchanges are scale, globalization, and multi-asset class capabilities. Exchanges are also trying to provide some block trading functionality and clearing mechanisms. Think about the challenges, especially the ones that Alasdair Haynes talked about with the Internet. When you take a closer look at exchanges, what are they?

The exchanges are really glorified networks. And these networks were once very expensive to build. That is why the market data companies acquired one another and grew large. Historically, the cost of connectivity, computing, and infrastructure is why exchanges needed scale. They were basically networks. Today, Moore's Law[4] and the Internet have made network computers more powerful and cheaper to build and have simplified the ability to connect. This created huge barriers to entry. Today, how do you grow a business when you can take three guys and a dog and create an exchange? Someone overnight can create a new business model and strip your flow faster than ever before.

Not only that, but your customers—banks and brokers—are also competing with exchanges by operating dark pools.[5] So, first, you need to sit with your clients on equal terms at the table. You heard earlier today that you can't just be a local player. When you are competing against Goldman Sachs, Morgan Stanley, and Credit Suisse, you are competing with strong global institutions. You need to have a very strong offering just to remain

[2] Alasdair Haynes is founder and, as of writing, CEO of Aquis Exchange. Before that he was at Chi-X Europe, representing this company at this conference.

[3] This refers to Chi-X Europe and other competitors.

[4] This is the idea that the number of transitors on integrated circuits doubles about every 2 years. Named after Intel co-founder, Gordon E. Moore, who wrote about this phenomenon in his 1960s paper.

[5] Alternative Trading Systems where orders are electronically matched in the "dark" and, most significantly, their size and price are not disclosed to other participants.

competitive. Scale also helps as an exchange. If you have one trading engine and run it across multiple geographies and asset classes, you can increase your scale and leverage. In addition, the more you can do in your factory the more locked in customers become. Going back to what Reto said about vertical integration,[6] you need to touch as many transactions across as much of the process as you can.

JOE ROSEN: I agree with everything my distinguished friend and colleague Larry said. I was engaged by my client Cisco Systems in a study for 2 years as an adviser to their team on global exchange competition.[7] It's an understatement to say that it was a super-hyper competitive space. I would say that you are not going to have organic growth. I am sure some of you don't want to hear that. The growth will come from acquisitions; and whether we will see five exchange groups or 15 dominating the industry, I don't know. Regardless, if you want market share, you will need to buy other exchange groups.

One of the points that emerged from our 50 interviews with senior executives during the Cisco study is the tension that now exists between broker-dealers—the former member-owners of the mutually-owned exchanges—and the exchange groups. The way competitive forces will also foster growth among exchanges is by each of them taking a bigger piece of the pie. That may be very tough going given the competition in this space. You got to think outside the box. That's a more strategic view. You have to obtain new products to list.

The exchanges have these massive engines to feed. You still have people to pay, and you're not going to be making much money at the margin. There is a patented mechanism for a system for trading risks, such as insurance liabilities, that cannot be traded now.[8] These are the actual liabilities themselves as opposed to CAT bonds.[9] This is something that melds the best of the

[6] Reto Francioni, CEO, Deutsche Börse AG, in his midday address at this conference.

[7] Rosen was senior adviser to the Cisco Global Exchange Survey. The extensive study and this survey led to the publication of The Competitive Landscape for Global Exchanges. What Exchanges Must Do to Meet User Expectations. Peter Robin, James Green. Foreward by Joe Rosen, Cisco Internet Business Solutions Group (IBSG), July 2008.

[8] This company is Extraordinary Re. Holdings, Inc. As of early 2014, Rosen was Chief Information Officer and Head of Capital Markets Relations at this company. See company website: http://xreholdings.com.

[9] Catastrophe, or CAT bonds, are high-yield debt instruments employed by insurance and reinsurance companies, governments and corporations (the "sponsors") to cover heavy losses that might arise from hurricanes, typhoons or other natural disasters including earthquakes. CAT bonds, first introduced in the mid-1990s, are not correlated with the global financial markets.

capital markets with our insurance markets. Any exchange group that is able to make such a partnership will be in a position to create huge volumes and transaction revenue for itself.

Maybe we were prescient. One of the suggestions that came out of the Cisco study is that exchange groups need to get much more into the technology business. We interviewed people at most of the exchanges. More and more of these exchange groups are, in effect, technology companies. And perhaps, who knows, maybe they will wind up competing with the Accentures and IBMs of the world. Stranger things can happen.

WEBER: Tim, you worked on an exchange floor back in 1979 as a summer intern. That's a fascinating span of time to observe these developments. Where do you see exchanges today compared with 1979?

TIM MAHONEY: The biggest change is the shift from people to systems. We too have just 40 something employees at BIDS Trading. So we have no expectations of competing directly with exchanges that are global Fortune 500 companies themselves. It is interesting to see how easy it is to compete with exchanges, around the edges, so to speak, in the price discovery phase. Exchanges have an enormous advantage in their scale of technology and infrastructure. If you want to be an exchange, you need to be a global player and in multiple asset classes. You must have a huge data infrastructure to do that. In fact, if the merger of NYSE and Deutsche Börse is approved and completed, they will have two huge global data bases—one in London and one in the United States.[10] The future of exchanges is about taking advantage of their scale.[11]

You need to diversify to become a dominant player. So, rather than compete with the broker-dealers, I would offer that exchanges should be providing scale infrastructure to the broker-dealer community because their business is more and more competitive. There is a lot of stuff broker-dealers are currently doing from a technology infrastructure and business perspective that you could facilitate. If they could outsource some of these technology

[10] On December 1, 2013, the European Commission announced that it was prohibiting the planned merger between Deutsche Börse AG and NYSE Euronext because, based on its definition of the market for derivatives trading, it considered the merger to be inadmissible under the law of competition.

[11] It is worth noting that the IntercontinentalExchange Group (ICE), the Atlanta-based operator of the second largest US futures market, confirmed its plans in late 2013 to dispose of key units in the NYSE Technologies business. That followed ICE's earlier acquisition of NYSE Euronext of which the business was a part. The NYSE Technologies units for sale reportedly included at the time of writing "infrastructure" and technology by NYFIX's network; the Appia messaging technology group; Wombat market data software; and the SuperFeed data dissemination business.

and business requirements to you, they would be in a much better spot. Exchanges could provide matching engine technology for broker's internalized crossing engines.

The natural entities to do all of this are exchanges. The exchanges will be globally positioned with tremendous infrastructure. The future for the exchange space is really to be the outsourced provider of secure, global infrastructure to the financial services firms, not just to the broker-dealer community. There is also no reason why you, as the exchange, could not be an outsourced provider to the banks. There is no reason you couldn't do it with the insurance companies. It's sort of like that proverbial sausage maker example: once you have the sausage maker built, all you want to do is put more and more stuff through it to make the sausages.

FRANK HATHEWAY: I think about the hierarchy of the outcomes—in other words, the return—that we can expect from different initiatives. We at NASDAQ look at expanding businesses. Everybody who runs a business does the same. How can we grow the size of the pie? How can we take bigger pieces of the pie? At the next level, we look at getting into new businesses. A lot of the new businesses that NASDAQ is interested in are indeed simply new to us. That said, these are not new businesses in an absolute sense. There are existing businesses in the commercial space. We do a lot of analysis of them along the lines of what Tim just said. We look at what is scalable. We ask, what is commoditized? Commoditized businesses are often scale businesses; scale is what we strive for. What serves the clients who we already serve on the data side, on the listing side, on the transaction side? Finally, we look at really new businesses. By that I mean *new* businesses in the sense of a product or service that doesn't exist anywhere else, not that's simply new to us. We bring buyers and sellers together, and provide people with information about that.

As Larry said, we need to work with the broad financial community. Exchanges can do this. The modern IPO is associated with NASDAQ. The Chicago Board Options Exchange leads for exchange-traded options. Growth markets are usually associated with London's AIM.[12] And at the AMEX it is ETFs.[13] If I had one on the tip of our tongue I wouldn't be saying

[12] The London Stock Exchange's market for smaller companies, it was formerly known as the Alternative Investment Market.

[13] On January 17, 2008, NYSE Euronext announced its acquisition of the AMEX for $260 million in stock, completing the deal in October. Before the closing of the acquisition, NYSE Euronext said AMEX would be renamed NYSE Alternext US. The name was changed again to NYSE Amex Equities in March 2009 and then to NYSE MKT LLC in May 2012.

it up here anyway. I would characterize what Larry, Joe and Tim said as the constraints and strengths that we face. I would apply them to this three-layer hierarchy—data, listings and transactions—that we could become involved in to grow.

PINAR EMIRDAG: I am responsible for running the business development team which is looking after six markets and 400-plus member clients at the London Stock Exchange. They include banks, HFT (high-frequency trading firms) and institutional clients. These clients cover a wide group. We cannot build anything and grow further without our clients' support. There are so many touch points with our clients across the London Stock Exchange Group. We are literally trying to meet and work with them, on everything from relationship management to business development.

We are building new types of platforms, new types of opportunities. It is what we are mandated to do.[14] We are involved in important thought leadership.[15] It is actually about innovation, a key to success at every business. Innovation is also important for credibility—if you don't innovate, you don't have credibility. If you don't have credibility you cannot build.

The next important thing is expanding into new geographies and new asset classes. In the equities space, expansion depends on technology. Innovation is more centered around technology today, it is more about new market models, and also data. For example, my team is looking after equities markets. Our job is to come up with new products. Within our team (and also outside the London Stock Exchange Group), we have three very public objectives. First, we are trying to get more efficient; two, we are trying to leverage all of the assets that we have; and third (this one is Economics 101): we are trying to do what many people in different types of industry are also trying to do—operate a strong business. But we are seeking to do it even better!

There is one last point I will leave you with (and this is a little controversial). I was recently talking to a hedge fund trader about what exchanges are doing, the good, the bad, the future of market structure, all that kind of stuff. He basically said, maybe we will all be trading on the Internet soon through some variant of a social network platform. This may be the future of exchanges!

[14] By late 2013, that strategy seemed to be working well for the London Stock Exchange. See, London Stock Exchange profit rises as diversification pays off. Kylie MacLellan, *Reuters,* November 13, 2013. http://uk.reuters.com/article/2013/11/13/uk-lse-results-idUKBRE9AC08020131113

[15] A thought leader is an individual or firm regarded as an expert and leader in a field.

WEBER: Ian, what is your take at ITG POSIT?[16] You developed one of the most successful early crossing networks. And you have gone on to innovate with a lot of advanced customer-facing technologies that augment the trading services coming from exchanges.

IAN DOMOWITZ: Back in 2007, just before MiFID[17] was implemented, Craig Donohue[18] made an interesting speech in Europe. He said the real competition is *not* between exchanges, it is between the exchanges and broker-dealers.

If you look globally and across different asset classes, and if you compile a list of what exchanges do, and compare that to what broker-dealers do—up to risking their capital—you get an almost perfect match of what each does today. That list is at least 16 items long. For example, there is managed financial networks on the broker side; network business on the exchange side. Both exchanges and brokers have gone global and multi-asset; both of them are technology providers; and brokers and exchanges offer trading decision support. On a fundamental level, they both offer execution services. The model for that diversification is in place and it has been implemented in one form or fashion as the exchanges have moved forward.

My second point relates more to what Pinar noted. I continue to believe that there is still competitive advantage to innovation. To some extent, I used to be in the exchange building business.[19] I can credibly tell you that there has been no fundamental change in the electronic exchange structure since Toronto's CATS system of 1977.[20] That's a long time ago.

We have a lot of cookie-cutter exchanges from the technology point of view. That does not mean that there hasn't been progress. Obviously, everything today is bigger, faster, and more scalable than before. There are more order types. For example, there is research out of UC- Berkeley showing how you can have systems that literally process billions of transactions in a second, compared with exchanges that process that many transactions in a day. The notion of congestion should be a thing of the past. That technology has not made it into the financial services industry.

[16] POSIT is ITG's anonymous electronic trade matching system.

[17] Markets in Financial Instruments Directive enacted in 2007 to harmonize financial service regulation and integrate markets more closely across the European Union.

[18] Craig Donahue was the former CEO of the CME Group. He was named executive chairman of OCC (formerly the Options Clearing Corporation) in September 2013.

[19] Prior to his career at ITG, Domotwitz, a noted academician, designed and implemented electronic exchanges throughout the world, including in the Middle East, India, Mexico, Czech Republic and the US.

[20] The Computer Assisted Trading System (CATS).

And where are the Amazon's and the Google's? There is a demand for analytics that are translated into exchange structure with a multi-assets orientation. Let's say you enter your 100,000-share order for Chuck E Cheese, what pops up? Well, just like Amazon, wouldn't you like to hedge this? Here is your hedge. Here is the combination of instruments to actually create the basket. However, that functionality does not exist yet. Yet we know that it is technologically possible; and that it has been implemented elsewhere.[21] So there is a role for technology here. You could call that infrastructure. But I think that it actually would be more disruptive than we think in terms of innovation.

WEBER: Ian, you pretty much painted a picture of a failure to innovate, or maybe it was a failure to see opportunities that have been exploited in other industries. Do you think that there is any fundamental reason why exchanges haven't done more since the CATS development in Toronto? Why didn't they push the envelope as far as, say, Amazon.com has? Is that a function of the impolite competition with their clients, the brokers? Is the answer that the brokers wouldn't want an exchange to have all those customer bells and whistles?

DOMOWITZ: No. I see it, not as a failure, but as an avenue. Any firm, one way or another, can concentrate on three things while doing only one of them superlatively. These three things are client intimacy—how well you know your client—efficiency and innovation. You may be able to point out companies that are leaders in all three simultaneously, but it is very difficult.

The way exchanges have innovated thus far is in terms of their business models. Business model innovation can trump technology almost any day of the week at certain stages in the cycle. We are looking at a very young industry. Demutualization only started back in the early 1990s and it was very slow. Demutualization started in the Nordic countries, Sweden being the first in 1993, and then it started to spread out from there. We didn't see it in the United States until very recently.

These firms have just now started to come to grips with what it means to operate as a corporate entity with stakeholders, but exchanges are now owned by people who expect a return. The exchanges have had to turn to business model innovation. The technology innovations that we have seen from exchanges are more in the area of client diversification. They have reached out to certain customer groups, such as the high-frequency trading community, to put in technology to attract that clientele. There is nothing wrong with that. That doesn't mean this is a failure; it just means that there is an opportunity.

[21] Amazon is the example Domowitz uses here.

WEBER: Ten or 20 years back, maybe just when demutualization was starting, exchanges were principally selling data, finding new companies that wanted to be listed, and charging trading fees. Open up an annual report today for most stock exchanges, and look at their cash equities business. For cash equities, those are still the three major revenue sources: Listing fees; selling market data and trading fees. Pinar, as you see things from where you are at the London Stock Exchange, will these new technologies and innovations with client groups lead to a fourth or fifth revenue source that the exchanges will be showing us in a few years? Where do you see the outcome of these exchange innovations and business model developments showing up?

EMIRDAG: I believe our clients' landscape is much more competitive than the landscape at the exchanges. We sometimes forget about this because we think that in Europe, for example, the landscape with the exchanges and the MTF's[22] really is small compared to all our clients' landscapes. A broker today is trying to get revenue across all the asset classes, and has global product offerings—it is actually quite tough out there for them. It also means that there are some activities that we can actually do that are beyond what you talked about. That's in terms, for instance, of working with our clients in the asset classes and the products that they are offering to their clients.

We can grow in that respect as well as in trading. When I think about trading fees, I mean that in the old days it was trading fees of cash equities and maybe some from data. Today we have an MTF business that handles corporate and government bonds in Europe. And we are looking into other asset classes as well. Trading fees today are not just cash equities trading fees. Imagine what the banks are doing in terms of their swap and hedging activities with their clients. We can proudly help them do some of those things much better.

One point that Rob Howe from Liquidnet made at this conference earlier, was about the information factor. Trading ideas are going all around the world. The world is changing. People should not necessarily be looking into trading healthcare in just one geography; they should be trading everything everywhere. In order to do that, they need real quality information. We are at the beginning of how exchanges should work in technology in this regard.

WEBER: Frank, is there going to be a bigger pie in the future for NASDAQ in terms of revenue? Is there a new slice or two that we should be anticipating?

[22] In Europe, a regulatory term for a non-exchange trading venue, known as a multilateral trading facility.

HATHEWAY: There will certainly be some new slices. I will go back to what Bruce Weber said at the beginning about share prices of exchanges underperforming the market. When we became public at NASDAQ, we were a monopoly that was being broken up. We were interested in thinking through what innovative ideas we could deliver. It turns out that we were better at delivering efficiencies than at delivering innovations. Now, oddly enough, our shares are being priced very much like a utility. Dependable cash flows, but that's about it.

Some say we are a utility. I don't think either point is quite right. We weren't the next Amazon.com back in 2005–2006. Nor are we Delmarva Power or Pepco utility companies right now. We are somewhere in between. We have already said we are expanding our trading exchange revenue sources of listing fees, data fees, transaction fees, and are going into the services area with an eye on scalable technology. We are good at providing commoditized products to member firms and issuers that deal with things that they assume they would not have to deal with. The fact that we are regulated brings our customers some comfort. The list of services we offer includes web services, news wire services, and a host of other things that benefit the investor relations function within a listed company.

On the trading side, there is SMARTS, a recent Australian acquisition,[23] and a monitoring and compliance service for high-frequency trading firms. And finally, we sell technology to 70 exchanges in 50 countries. In a way, that is how we get at Larry's global scale issue.

So you have a lot of challenges in member-exchange relationships and in the exchange sovereign government relationship. It makes it difficult to actually own an exchange every place in the world. If you want scale, and indeed you want to get some of the "scale return" from building trading systems, then why not sell it to exchanges around the world? That, in fact, is what we do. That has grown from simply selling the matching engine (which is what we use to do) to selling other things like data services.

How do you run a data business? We are efficient and pretty good at it, and we have a new business starting up to do this. We will help other exchanges around the world run their data business better. We can show them how much more revenue they could get.

WEBER: It certainly sounds like the pie chart will change in a couple of years. Tim, what about the competition between broker-dealers and exchanges that Ian was talking about? Is that an accurate characterization?

[23] On July 27, 2010, NASDAQ OMX Group, Inc. signed an agreement to acquire SMARTS Group, a technology provider of market surveillance solutions to exchanges, regulators and brokers.

MAHONEY: Take BIDS. Our company was formed by a broker-dealer consortium to compete directly with the exchanges. Think about BATS. BATS was formed and Direct Edge was formed, both to challenge the for-profit duopoly.[24] Go back to 2005–2006 and consider Reg NMS[25] and a bunch of other factors in this context. The broker-dealer community and the regional exchanges created their own ECNs. They took a series of steps to be competitive against a duopoly where pricing was controlled.[26]

At this point, the realization is that you do not have to control a matching function as a commoditized product. I don't think that there is any longer a fear that we will be in this spot where either NASDAQ or New York, or anyone else, will be controlling the pricing at the point of sale.[27] I think that they've transformed their view on it.

If you had a 13-year old son or daughter and they came to you and said, gee dad, when I grow up should I go work for a broker-dealer firm? I would say no. If you were engaged in strategy for an exchange, I think you would find the same kind of concept. If someone's child aspires to be a broker-dealer, I can see that parent saying, no honey go do something else when you grow up! I think a lot about Jim Collins' book, *Good to Great.*[28] When he talks about a great company, you are either a hedge hog or a fox in this

[24] The for-profit duopoly refers to the New York Stock Exchange and NASDAQ being the dominant trading markets in US equities prior to the advent of competition from alternative trading systems and other competitors.

[25] Regulation National Market System (NMS) was approved by the Securities and Exchange Commission in 2005 and introduced 2 years later to further advance the ideas of a national market system. The regulation includes the order protection, or trade through rule; access rule (fair access) to market data including quotations; rules on sub-penny trading and on market data specifically.

[26] This is a veiled reference to how dealers and market makers reputedly kept spreads much wider and kept them "fixed" in the duopoly model until new regulations such as the order handling rules forced more active price-quote competition.

[27] This refers to how the brokers had once feared the pricing power of the duopoly, NYSE and NASDAQ. In the competitive environment under discussion at this conference that should be less of a concern, Mahoney argued. Of course, this ties into US securities regulations from the order handling rules to Reg NMS that effectively removed the kind of "control" the speaker is referring to.

[28] Good to Great: Why Some Companies Make the Leap... and Others Don't. Jim Collins (William Collins, October 16, 2001). Collins describes how companies make the transition from being "average" to "great" and how some fail to reach that height.

journey to become a great company.[29] The exchanges have demonstrated this tremendous hedgehog-like ability to survive and succeed. And I believe that this can be traced back to their infrastructure.

One thing we know for certain—data are going to be important. You are going to need infrastructure to support that. Think about cloud technology, and the demands on a wide variety of people about how they manage the data. We can compete real effectively at the point of sale and matching. I compete with Ian. However, to keep my costs down, I rely on scale from multiple providers. I can't have my own data center. I know that during the recent hurricane everyone was worried about the potential impact on our data center. Our data center is operating 24 × 4; it has three back-up engines and everything else. Unless there is a direct nuclear hit it can keep going! Which is good to know. Our exchange will be up whether you are up or not. That is where there is a huge advantage. You can't do that on your own.

WEBER: It sounds like from your perspective, Tim, that there is a kind of symbiotic relationship here in the value chain with exchanges as Isaiah Berlin's hedgehogs doing one or two basic things well, and broker-dealers and nimble systems like BIDS as foxes, swiftly combing ideas and features to serve traders?

MAHONEY: Yes. We've figured out where that is. I don't deny it. There is a small but important space that provides highly customized services to institutional investors. These are too small of an opportunity for a big exchange, though they can still enjoy efficiencies that a single broker could not replicate on their own.

[29] Mahoney, in a follow-up for this chapter, recalled the ancient Greek parable that distinguishes between foxes which, according to one poet of this great period, "knows many small things, and hedgehogs, which know one big thing." The parable was developed into a famous essay by Sir Isaiah Berlin in 1953 and the idea was extolled in Collins' book. In his book, Collins characterizes the good to great leaders who go onto succeed as "hedgehogs"—with their singular ideas of overarching importance. Collins distinguishes between the hedgehog, laser focused on one idea, and the "clever" fox, circling the hedgehog's den, constantly coming up with new ideas to "eat" the hedgehog. The fox simply does not see the world through the lens of a single idea.

As Mahoney elaborated, the hedgehog successfully knows how to simplify and boil down a complex world into a single, organizing principle—the kind of basic principle that unifies, organizes, and guides all decisions. Hedgehogs though are not simplistic. They can be compared to the great thinkers, Mahoney recalled, a group who turned complexity into simple, yet profound, ideas. (For example, Adam Smith and the invisible hand; Darwin and evolution). Thus leaders of good-to-great companies develop a Hedgehog Concept that is seemingly simple but, in fact, reflects penetrating insight and sharp understanding.

WEBER: Joe, you have a background on the exchange side and also on the technology side. Would you encourage a rookie in the industry to go into the broker-dealer space, the exchange space, the IT space, or just run away?

ROSEN: The IT space. I basically agree with almost everything I've heard on this panel. It seems like we are all coming to the same conclusion, so please stay with me for a few moments.

Frank, it seems you guys actually did listen to one of the recommendations in the Cisco study—namely to basically get into IT, into technology consulting which is what you are doing. Tim, you are talking about outsourcing. You are also talking about commoditization. You are talking about the matching engine itself as a commodity. I would venture to say that, if you take this to the logical extreme, you are saying that the equity trading platform, including yours, is becoming a utility.

You know with the acquisitions made both by NYSE Euronext and NASDAQ OMX, that this is the route of vertical integration. I believe that regulators today will never let that completely happen. You can make an argument that it is all about cost. Everyone wants to trade at the lowest cost available, assuming that everything else works and that it is reliable, and so on. You can make the argument that a move to vertical integration—a 'cradle to grave' approach—is inevitable. I know this will never happen. Call it whatever company you want—NYSE Euronext, Goldman Sachs, Amazon, and Oracle all together.

This is the new infrastructure. We will take you public. We will manage your money. We will do the execution. We will do the clearing and settlement. I know that this will never happen, at least not in my lifetime (and I hope to live to be 120!). But if you take the logical view, it's a cost-based business. When you are talking about commodities and utilities that is what it is. That is maybe where you should be going. We know that the plumbing and the back-end are different from the front-end but it is hard to do it well. DTCC[30] is the utility, it is the plumbing for this industry. For equities it works well, especially compared to Europe. Why is this?

Because it's a natural monopoly. Their economies of scale work real well. You can make a very good argument for a monopoly if you want to drive the cost down. And that is where we are heading. It is so funny. Before the 2007 financial meltdown, the US Justice and Treasury Departments were about to jump on the CME, and say, 'You have got to get rid of this anti-competitive vertical silo.[31] I am not saying that the CME caused the meltdown, but

[30] Depository Trust and Clearing Corporation.

[31] Rosen is referring to the vertical silo at CME with its front and back-end platforms, including the execution and processing of transactions.

obviously people were focusing on other things. No one has heard a peep about any of those studies since then. Who knows if it is ever going to happen. Now everyone is talking about how, oh yeah, a vertical silo is good. It's safe and all that. I am not making a value judgment in either case.

But ultimately there will be a lot more. I think a lot more consolidation is needed. So maybe it's an NYSE Euronext, Goldman Sachs and Oracle that get it together, or NASDAQ OMX with these others. I know it sounds outlandish. But that is my short answer, Bruce.

WEBER: That's an impressive forecast Joe, thanks. Larry, which of these exchanges will reward their shareholders in the next 5 years and why?

TABB: A lot of what everyone said is absolutely accurate. The issue is a scale game with the three pillars—listings, market data and transaction services. However, these three pillars won't be enough in the future. A technology structure is also needed. The idea of offering data co-location services makes a lot of sense if you are looking at issues under Basel III[32] that call for more bank capital. Banks' profitability has been under attack. Brokers dealers will need to rethink and restructure their cost basis. They are not going to have the bespoke infrastructure that they had before. They are not going to have the huge data centers they had before. They need to look to partners to do what they have to get done, especially in the more commodity-type products.

Under Dodd-Frank and at Basel III every major profit center is really under attack. The regulators don't seem to want to stop the banks from taking risk. As regulators de-risk the banks, it hurts profitability. The only thing the regulators seem okay with is for these large banks to handle transactions as an agent and not as a principal. This basically turns all the banks into agency brokers as they jettison their prop trading businesses, and ambiguity around the Volcker Rule[33] puts constraints on market making. I don't think that is a good idea. If banks can't easily take principal risk, it means that the banks need to think about cost and the value they add. Exchanges could be very good partners to exchanges in this situation as it could push banks to sign up for their third-party services.

DOMOWITZ: Part of the point is missed. It is true that competition on the basis of matching is a cost game, and that scalability certainly applies. The original point related to vertical integration is not quite the same.[34] If you

[32] The Third Basel Accord of global voluntary regulatory standards on capital requirements, liquidity and stress testing.

[33] Part of the Dodd-Frank Act, the Volcker Rule prohibits banks from proprietary trading activities.

[34] See, Rosen's comment on the acquisitions of both NYSE Euronext and NASDAQ OMX.

have stockholders, and you are operating a commoditized business with low margins, then you have to move into areas that have higher margins. In one way or another, broker-dealers have been doing this for 10 years. It is a content game as much as anything else. Content still has value. The marginal value of information may be zero, but the average value will be positive. That is a data issue. But the marginal value of added content is often incalculable. However, we do have the exchanges, broadly defined, moving into content as well.[35]

The exchanges have moved into managed financial networks. They talk about outsourcing the technology. This isn't just a question of creating new verticals around clearance and the commoditized part of the business as they move into other areas. This is a question of searching for new areas of business, and there is an easy model to follow. That is, the broker-dealer which, in turn, has been adapting to what the institutional buy-side has been up to for the last 10 years.[36]

The business has changed because of the buy side-trading desk. Tim is right, there was a point when the notion of brokers competing with exchanges was all about the matching system. That is no longer the case. The broker-dealers have had to deal with this fact. The buy-side has been looking for everything the sell-side can offer, from technology in the form of execution management, order management, and managed financial networks, to the analytics side of trading, whether that be pre- or post- trade (and this entails algorithm development).

Have you heard of exchanges developing algorithms? I have.[37] They are both users and developers. The data game is certainly an old game in the exchange space. The value-added content game is a new one. But the exchanges are there, as are the broker-dealers.

It is not just building upwards—it is also building outwards.[38] That is something that seems to have been missed in some of these comments today. To me, commoditization is the driver. Commoditization is driving a lot of this

[35] Transaction cost analysis, for example.

[36] Back in the mid-1990s, "trading" staff at the trading desks on the institutional buy-side were essentially regarded as clerks and order takers. That changed with regulatory changes and advances in technology with buy-side desks evolving into full-fledged trading operations that "added value" with sophisticated analytics, processes and procedures. Brokers, in turn, adapted to the demands of the new look buy-side trading desks.

[37] NASDAQ, for example, was unsuccessful in its efforts to promote its VWAP and TWAP algorithms.

[38] Diversification is another way of putting this, says Domowitz.

because you have shareholders and they want margins. They want margins, and they need a new way to make them.

MAHONEY: The value-added content is, almost by definition, not scalable—it is the unscalable piece of it. The delivery mechanism very well could be scalable. I just have a hard time seeing exchanges getting into value-added content. The delivery mechanism is for sure something they could do.

DOMOWITZ: Tim, this is a question about defining content, right?

MAHONEY: Yes, yes.

DOMOWITZ: So give me a definition?

MAHONEY: Primary research.

DOMOWITZ: Got it. So-called fundamental research is a game that I have not seen exchanges getting into. However, I have found exchanges that have started to act as research aggregators. We have research aggregators in much the same way we think about liquidity aggregators. They have found a way into that space. But in my mind, the content is broader. As Tim knows very well, part of the business I run has to do with the transaction cost analysis of pre- and post- trade trading performance. I have seen that on the exchanges as well. They do it for a variety of reasons, and they are in various stages of development. But that is also content. When people pay us for that, they are paying for content. Is that scalable? The answer is both yes and no.

MAHONEY: And data?

DOMOWITZ: And data, yes that is right.

MAHONEY: The hardest part of data is getting that clean tick data from around the world.

DOMOWITZ: Exactly. So you have a transformation, for example, in the world of transaction cost analysis (TCA), where the connection between the financial network and actually analyzing trading performance is getting closer and closer together to the point where the network model might as well be the TCA analyzer.[39] The exchanges are well positioned for that for obvious reasons—and some have maybe even gone there. I am thinking of content more broadly defined, where there are scalable pieces and there are those that can't be adapted to the exchange structure.

TABB: I agree with you whole-heartedly. A lot of exchanges don't have the customer order, and don't know if that one hundred share order is really only one hundred shares or if that order is really a hundred-share pieces of a hundred thousand share order. While some exchanges have the front-end technology that can help put the order in context, if you only have the

[39] The concept is more easily understood by recognizing that with more users on a financial network, there is also more information and more feedback so that the network becomes more analytically attuned.

matching engine, it becomes really hard to understand the totality of the information and what goes with what.

DOMOWITZ: I have a dirty little secret for you. Broker-dealers have the same problem. They have the same problem because order management systems, or OMSs, don't speak to execution management systems, or EMSs. If you are looking at the OMS, you don't have the granularity to think about the trading strategies. If you are looking at the EMS, you are only looking at child orders.[40] Everybody has this problem, and someone will solve it. When they do, everybody will have it and will share technology.

MAHONEY: In fact, exchanges are in the best positions to tackle this. They are large global players with scalable infrastructure.

WEBER: Joe, Frank and Pinar—I want to ask the three of you about the fine line between value-added content and the raw material for these aggregators?

ROSEN: I wanted to comment on TCA. ITG is great at it. I mean you guys are leaders, but I certainly wouldn't say it is a commodity. On the other hand, you are not the only ones who are providing TCA services. I am not sure how much premium you can price in there. I am not privy to your pricing models. It is obviously not commoditized to the extent that the plain-vanilla execution is. But I would question how much. If you have other examples of what you guys are using, you probably do not want to talk about it if you are charging premium prices.

MAHONEY: The arrival price strategy, you know, the models you use for predictive purposes, is truly the intellectual property that you have.[41]

DOMOWITZ: And scalable.

MAHONEY: I forget what yours is called. Whatever the model is?

DOMOWITZ: ACE.

MAHONEY: ACE is an IP[42] you can't mess around with.

WEBER: Frank and Pinar, from the exchange perspective, is there this fine line out there between content that will help you grow your business, and the content that is best left to other rivals and competitors?

[40] For a closer look at "child orders," this excerpt from *Future Magazine* is helpful. "The role of the high-frequency algo trading system, however, is not to trade the trend, but to enter and exit the market as frequently as possible for miniscule individual profits in a range environment. It does this by identifying what have become known as "child orders." These are large orders that have been chopped down into small, minor orders, partly to hide the order's footprint and partly to avoid disturbing the market's existing liquidity and driving price away from intended execution levels." Algo trading in the liquidity mirage of high-frequency trading. Alex Benjamin, May 1, 2011, *Futures Magazine*

[41] Mahoney is referring to ITG's TCA product.

[42] Internet Protocol.

HATHEWAY: That is a fairly clear and practical line. We can see what is going on cross-sectionally that an individual broker cannot see. We cannot see what is going on over the life of an order. When we try to provide additional granularly about the market in terms of data products, we exploit our ability to see what is going on cross-sectionally. There exists other products that did not take off and, in hindsight, were outside what an exchange can do. For example, we initiated a project—the Independent Research Network—facilitating the provision of research reports for small companies that did not have research analysts following them from the brokerage community. But we are not doing that any longer. The capability for the exchanges to get into some of the enhanced value content business that Ian was referring to is certainly there.

I don't think it is a fine line between what we can do and what the brokers can do. At least for us within the NASDAQ OMX space, it is a pretty clear line. There are areas where we have a relatively clear advantage, and there are areas where we do not.

EMIRDAG: Let's think about our universe, about market structure, and the world of exchanges. This includes competitors of exchanges, the clients of exchanges, and the technology providers. It is an equity system. There are a lot of things that people do at different phases in the equity system, and they do these things for different reasons. There are lots of opportunities in this marketplace to build something valuable without necessarily stepping on each other's toes. I still think that I can work with our clients and find things that they themselves do not necessarily need to do anymore. The work has changed. We should be on top of this, this is our job. This is what we are getting paid for. We need to understand how the work changes. What is going on between banks? What do they want to do these days? What do they not want to do, both 1 year from now and 5 days from now. The same goes for us. The same goes for some of the technology vendors. This universe is full of opportunities.

Having said that, this is all sounding rosy. Even though something is commoditized honestly, you are still competing. That doesn't mean that your life is the people who are actually running the exchange or the people that are actually in your business. We are thinking about these things every day. And now what is the next non-commoditized, let's say business? The business is not really unique either. It simply requires lots of innovation and very good planning.

WEBER: Yes, a lot of commodity prices have risen sharply over the past 2 or 3 years. Exchange trading fees have gone down so you are right about commodities. Are there any questions from the audience?

WAYNE ARDEN [Independent Consultant]: All of the US exchanges are regulated by the SEC, and they are under margin pressure to varying degrees. They have diversified into other asset classes. Why do you think that the US exchanges haven't diversified into fixed income? If you look at firms that are in fixed income, they are global and they are successful. Firms like ICAP, GFI Group and Cantor Fitzgerald. Fixed income is a sister class to stock; arguably it is an easier class than credit derivatives or interest rate derivatives. Why do you think the US exchanges haven't gone in that direction?

TABB: Historically, the challenge with fixed-income instruments is that they don't trade very often. There are millions of issues, if you include munies and mortgages. There are some 30,000 corporate bonds. If they trade once a week, that's a lot of trading. How do you fit a typically fixed-income market that developed as an over the counter model with folks who have capital, who can inventory bonds, into a stock exchange model? Dealers can buy bonds from folks who want to sell them. That has typically been the role of the dealer. New York created a corporate bond market, they recently reinvested in it, and I understand it is actually starting to get some traction.[43]

To a certain extent, the exchanges want to stay out of the capital game that dealers have had. The number of prime dealers over the years has declined. It hasn't been a volume infrastructure game. It has been more of a capital game, so to speak, where dealers buy low and sell high. That typically doesn't align well with the exchange moded that takes a small transaction fee from each trade.

MAHONEY: Principal-based trading can still make sense, and dealers are still going to make markets in securities where the spreads are wide enough. NASDAQ was a spread market prior to 2001.[44] When the market moved to decimal pricing in that year, the entire market became agency-based within 6 months. My guess is that as long as the spreads are wide enough, and on a scale where you can make money for the broker-dealers and the banks, they will continue to do it. In FX,[45] it is still much that way too.

TABB: The new MiFID fixed-income rule is actually supposed to migrate to a limit order book. We will see if that actually happens, but that is the way MiFID is written.

[43] In 2007, the New York Stock Exchange revamped and relaunched its bond trading market following an exemption from the Securities and Exchange Commission providing the exchange approval to trade corporate debt, convertibles, foreign bank and government bonds, US Treasury and agency securities, municipals and debt-based structured products.

[44] The US equities markets switched from fractional to decimalized pricing in 2001 following the introduction of the order handling rules in 1997.

[45] Foreign exchange market.

HATHEWAY: Here in the US, NASDAQ actually runs the fixed-income reporting system for FINRA. Fixed income securities are not something we have ever got into running with a transaction system in either place. Regulation in the US is such that when NASDAQ considers treasury securities (and I would include treasury derivatives), they have a different regulator—not the SEC but the CFTC. So that in Europe or at least in Stockholm where it is a bit more uniform in terms of who the regulatory authority is. We do all these things, corporate fixed income, sovereign debt, fixed-income derivatives, over there, but here in the states we do not. We will watch New York, but it doesn't seem to be something that we will be jumping into real soon.

ALLEN GRODY [Financial InterGroup]: I have not heard anyone talk about something that could potentially be a huge new opportunity, a whole new world of potential retail products within this whole new electronic world of swaps.[46]

HATHEWAY: We have a majority stake in a subsidiary. IDCG that is active in the swap area.[47] A lot of the future for swaps is dependent on regulation. We have been talking about swaps for 2 years. I decided that I would leave it off today until we get some clarity on regulation.

ALLEN GRODY: Thoughts from the panel on Dodd-Frank?

HATHEWAY: Obviously, the jury is still out on many dimensions of Dodd-Frank. It's clear on how the process works. We just talked about swaps, and there is a whole host of other things at stake here, including the consumer protection part of it, along with the other regulations. Dodd-Frank made some pretty strong statements about the importance of transparency, and we think, as an exchange operator, that is great. But how it gets put into practice will have the more telling impact on our business.

TABB: Dodd-Frank will probably be pretty good for exchanges. There is pressure on the clearing organizations not to be owned by the banks, to be separately owned. You see the LSE looking like a strong bid for LCH. Clearnet, but who knows what is going to happen.[48] And there is pressure

[46] This refers to trading on interest rates swaps in US dollars, euros and sterling that commenced trading on electronic swap execution facilities, or SEFs, in early 2014 as part of the changes mandated by Dodd-Frank 3 years earlier. See, Market unflustered by SEF Big Bang. Mike Kentz. *Reuters*, February 14, 2014. http://www.reuters.com/article/2014/02/14/swaps-trading-idUSL5N0LJ3WW20140214

[47] As of writing that ownership stake had changed. See, LCH Buys IDCG, US Swaps Clearinghouse from Nasdaq. Nandini Sukumar, *Bloomberg*. August 15, 2001. http://www.bloomberg.com/news/2012-08-15/lch-buys-idcg-u-s-swaps-clearinghouse-from-nasdaq.html

[48] As of early 2014, the London Stock Exchange owned a majority stake in clearinghouse LCH.Clearnet after completing its acquisition in May 2013.

for the over-the-counter markets to move to SEF trading. There is a lot of competition, especially with the inter-dealer brokers who were there. But it looks a lot more like an exchange than it does an over the counter market. As Frank said, the rules aren't dry. In fact, they aren't even written yet, so it is hard to tell.

But the market overall looks more like an agency SEF, centrally cleared market than a capital-driven OTC market. It should be good for exchanges or exchange-like products. It may take 20 years for the SEF's to carve up the business and for the exchanges to buy all that business up. In the long run, it is probably good for an exchange and an exchange-like entity.

SHANTARAM HEGDE [University of Connecticut]: Where do you see growth opportunities in banking and insurance companies? Who are your major consumers of the trading services you provide? Will there be a new regime where banking, insurance, and trading will be conducted under the same roof?

TABB: Doing more trading with other types of bank products and insurance products?

I think a lot of firms do that already. Now tie in exchanges. I feel like the exchanges are wonderful places to be—the cloud service providers for the industry. You know they are secure and semi trusted. They are big data centers.

WEBER: Very diplomatic Larry.

HATHEWAY: They haven't been indicted lately.

TABB: The writing is on the wall for the proprietary data center. It will be gone. It will be natural for a lot of that stuff to wind up closer to the exchange where you can get great economies of scale. If it winds up being that way, why not also put in some of your banking technology and insurance data service issue, service providers, and perhaps some other things in as well. That is especially so if the exchanges are global, and if they have a network around the world and around the clock.

HATHEWAY: Another answer to that is to think about how small we are. We at NASDAQ are a 2,500-people worldwide company. There are six hundred people in the exchange business in the US for listing, for data, for transactions, for overhead. We don't have the staff to run a large relationship business. That is really what you are talking about when you are thinking about calling on insurance companies and banks and pension funds, public pension funds and everything else. I will leave that kind of thing to others who have a hundred times as many people as we have.

ROSEN: There is one more potential revenue source we didn't really mention. It was alluded to in an earlier panel, and some of you will say I am crazy. At some point, exchanges will be charging for bandwidth, particularly for too many quotes and excessive cancellations.[49] I know it is a topic that has been discussed. Most people say it will never happen. However, if you do it and someone else also does it, are participants going to trade elsewhere? Maybe the regulators will come to this idea? Finally, it will be interesting to see how this whole new net neutrality issue plays out, insofar as what I allude to here could become a potential revenue source going forward.[50] This idea, by the way, is mentioned in the Cisco study.

WEBER: Thank you, panelists. I may be the Dean at Lerner College, but I have to defer to Bob, the conference Chair.

SCHWARTZ: This has been a fascinating panel and I learned a lot from it. I have one thing to add. Larry, I heard you say something about three men, a dog and a computer. Well, it is only one man, a dog and a computer. Do you all know what the functions of each are? The computer makes the trades. The man feeds the dog. And the dog keeps the man away from the computer! [Laughter]

Thank you.

[49] Rosen is referring to the imposition of fees on trading participants who enter multiple trades over and over again and then ultimately cancel most of them. This trading activity strains the execution provider's network and in effect, "taxes" the provider's services. The argument is that the "excessive" quoting and trading participant should be charged for imposing this strain on "bandwidth."

[50] "Net neutrality" is the idea that an exchange does not discriminate against a range of trading participants and content providers.

CHAPTER 6: IPO CAPITAL RAISING IN THE GLOBAL ECONOMY

Moderator: David Weild, *IssuWorks, Inc.*
Gregory L. Wright, *ThinkEquity LLC*
Barry E. Silbert, *SecondMarket Inc.*
Hüseyin Erkan, *Istanbul Stock Exchange*
Joseph Hall, *Davis, Polk & Wardwell LLP*
Steve Wunsch, *Wunsch Auction Systems*

ROBERT SCHWARTZ: When I think about an exchange and, more broadly, about a securities marketplace, I am reminded of the secondary market for trading shares. Of course, you need liquidity in the secondary market so people will be willing to buy newly-issued shares. Now let's put that in the context of a broader macro economy. Why do we want a liquid, secondary market? Answer: It is terribly important for capital raising. The exchanges are part of a broader mechanism for capital raising. Who better than David Weild to moderate this superb panel on this topic. Dave, what is happening on the IPO front?

DAVID WEILD: Steve Wunsch, the founder of the Arizona Stock Exchange, landed this topic on Bob's radar screen. Steve is on our panel. Let me note that our company published several important studies on this topic that lawmakers cited on the U.S. Senate floor and in a number of Congressional letters. One is *A Wakeup Call for America.*[1] This was the first study that tabulated the number of historical corporate listings on the U.S. and other major stock markets. It observed a steep drop in the population of listed companies in the United States. A separate study documented a steep decline in U.S. IPOs. We titled the first release of this study, *Why are IPO's in the ICU?*[2] That title wasn't sharp enough, so our subsequent and final version was retitled, *Market Structure*

[1] A wake-up call for America. David Weild and Edward Kim, Grant Thonton, November 2009.

[2] Why are IPOs in the ICU? David Weild and Edward Kim, Grant Thornton.

R.A. Schwartz et al. (eds.), *The Economic Function of a Stock Exchange*, Zicklin School of Business Financial Markets Series, DOI 10.1007/978-3-319-10350-1_6

is Causing the IPO Crisis - and More.[3] This version linked the IPO crisis to unemployment and it set off a firestorm of interest following publication.

Our panel has other excellent and thought-provoking industry professionals. Gregory Wright, CEO of ThinkEquity, is a dear friend. ThinkEquity is a specialist firm focused on technology, healthcare, investment banking, and equity research. Barry Silbert, founder and CEO of Second Market, is pioneering a liquidity solution for corporations in the private equity markets. His company has put up trades in the securities of private companies including LinkedIn and Facebook. Hüseyin Erkin came here all the way from Istanbul. I understand, Hüseyin, you were a former student of Professor Schwartz. Today, Hüseyin is CEO of the Istanbul Stock Exchange.[4] How impressive. I would like to get his perspective shortly because the Istanbul Stock Exchange model is a bit different than the stock exchange model in the U.S. Joseph Hall, a partner at Davis, Polk & Wardwell, is a corporate securities attorney. Joe spent time at the SEC on policy matters and for former SEC Chairman Bill Donaldson.

I was at NASDAQ until 2003, spending 4 years as vice chairman and executive vice president in charge of its listing businesses. I later founded a boutique called Capital Markets Advisor Partners, LLC, now IssuWorks, Inc., that today uses technology to help issuers and investment banks reach a much larger number of qualified institutional buyers.

Let me begin. There are now four bills in Congress[5] that address the critical issue of capital formation. Before I get into that, I have a pet peeve about the group attending here today! It is that most of the conference's

[3] Market Structure is Causing the IPO Crisis - and More. David Weild and Edward Kim, Grant Thornton, June 2010.

[4] Hüseyin Erkan, CEO of the World Federation of Exchanges at the time of writing, was the Chairman and CEO of the Istanbul Stock Exchange from 2007 until 2012. He graduated from New York University Stern Business School with a B.S. degree in Economics (1981) and an MBA in the fields of International Business and Finance (1984). His thesis project was on currency risk management at the United Nations Development Program.

[5] The Conference took place in late 2011. The JOBS Act was signed into law by President Obama on April 5, 2012 in the Rose Garden, bringing these bills together. David Weild was among the attendees. The four bills, Titles, I, II, III and IV of the Act, are credited with giving birth to such changes as the new IPO classification of an Emerging Growth Company. That permits Confidential Filings with the SEC and Testing the Waters (pre-IPO). It also required the SEC to study the impact of decimalization on capital formation. Title II repealed the "Prohibition against general solicitation" of private placements and subsequently led to crowdfunding for accredited investors. Title III, as of the end of 2013, still had not seen rules issued by the SEC. It was intended to allow crowdfunding of securities to public investors. Title IV, popularly called Reg. A+, will allow a lower cost "IPO lite," offering of up to $50 million in securities to the public.

participants focus on S&P 500 issues and largely ignore what is happening in the broader market. In fact, the vast majority of publicly-listed companies trade nothing like companies on the S&P 500 which consists of the largest of the large-cap stocks. Yet the median equity market value of a publically-listed company in the United States is a micro-cap stock with a market value of only $450 million. So, when you ask, 'Who are we optimizing these markets for?' we need to understand that almost all analysis is focused on trading data, volume data, and liquidity data showing improvements for S&P 500 stocks. There is a world of difference between large-cap stocks and the vast majority of publicly-listed stocks that are small-cap (sub-$2 billion in market value), micro-cap (sub-$500 million in market value), and nano-cap (sub-$100 million in market value).

How can we support small and micro-cap stocks, how can we help companies go public? Are we doing enough? Have we entirely lost sight of what, fundamentally, markets are supposed to do? That is to get capital to businesses that deserve that capital if you will, and that create jobs. Is there an ideological war raging over the role of markets? On the one hand, there are no market intermediaries today like we had in the former NASDAQ and NYSE models of market makers and specialists. Trading costs have practically dropped to zero and trading focused, theme-driven (think ETF) and index strategies—as opposed to single stock selection—have risen to a level that may be undermining capital formation. If everything was displaced by exchange-traded funds, there would no more stock analysts and stock brokers required to value individual companies.

This is U.S. data (Exhibit 6.1). The purple tranche is sub-$50 million IPOs from 1991 and to 2011. You can see how the small IPOs once accounted for 80% of the market. That fell off a cliff in 1997 and 1998—before Sarbanes-Oxley in 2002.[6] The convenient whipping boy is that increased costs to issuers, caused by Sarbanes-Oxley, triggered the decline in small IPOs. But as you can see from the data, the real drop-off in small IPOs occurred all the way back to 1998 with the implementation of electronic stock markets with Reg. ATS.[7] That was on the heels of the Order Handling

[6] The Sarbanes-Oxley Act of 2002, named after U.S. Senator Paul Sarbanes and U.S. Representative Michael Oxley, the main architects, introduced major changes to the regulation of financial practice and corporate governance in the United States.

[7] Reg. ATS, introduced by the SEC in 1998, aims to protect investors and regulate this type of trading system. As of writing, the regulation had strict record keeping and reporting requirements on areas such as transparency once an ATS reaches more than five percent of the trading volume in any security. Examples of ATSs include Electronic Communication Networks (ECNs), crossing networks and call markets.

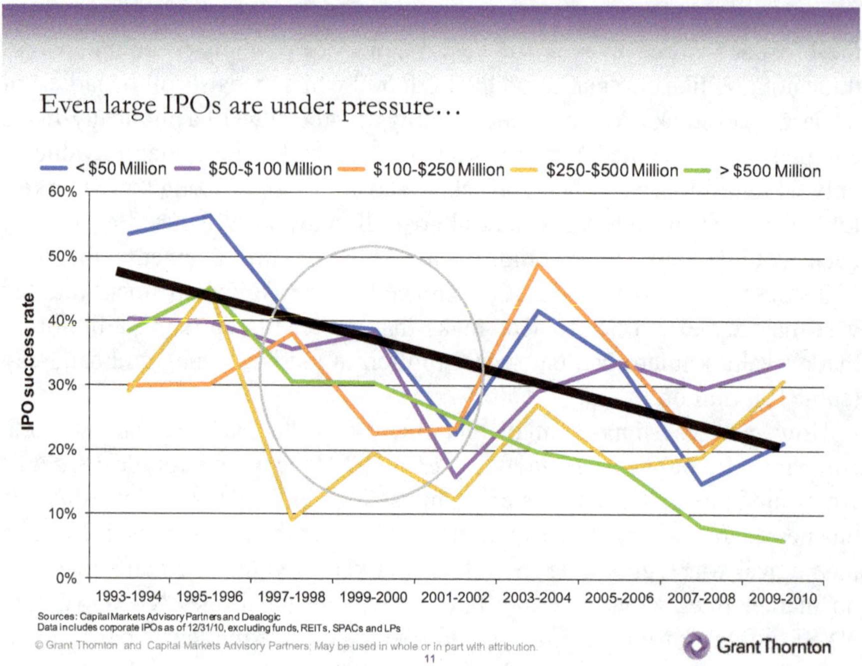

Exhibit 6.1 IPO success rate (United States)

Rules of 1997.[8] The United States decimated the small IPO market well before Sarbanes-Oxley and the introduction of decimalization in 2001[9] were enacted.

Once again, the trend started to accelerate with the implementation of the Order Handling Rules and Regulation ATS in 1998. These two rules really gave birth to electronic order books and electronic stock execution. These changes, combined with decimalization, collapsed the profitability of small-cap trading, research and sales for small broker dealers. Subsequently, this caused the collapse of the small public company listing business in the

[8] The Order Handling Rules (OHR) significantly changed the economic structure of trading stocks for dealers and specialists in the U.S., narrowing spreads in stock trading. The limit order display rule and the quote rule, key features of the rules, were introduced in the wake of well-publicized charges of price collusion on the dealer markets, which led to a regulatory settlement with NASDAQ.
See background on OHR, http://www.stock-market-investors.com/stock-strategies-and-systems/sec-order-handling-rules.html

[9] Stock trading in the U.S. switched from fractional increments to decimal pricing.

United States. Many would say it once made the U.S. stock markets the envy of stock markets around the world.

I want to start in a moment with Hüseyin for some of the Istanbul perspective on how electronic markets helped or hurt the U.S. economy. From a broad European perspective, is the U.S. stock market still the envy of the world? I posed this question, when I was in London recently, to a number of European investors, market professionals and regulators. After we hear from Hüseyin, I will share a little bit of their feedback about what they envy and find disturbing.

HÜSEYIN ERKAN: Many companies came to the United States to conduct public offerings and to raise capital for themselves. The NYSE was once the largest stock exchange for international issues, competing with London. The NYSE was competitive in both listings as well as in the number of shares traded. There were multiple levels of listings. The SEC was very keen on regulating what was traded, what was made public, or what was sold to the public in the United States. When we look back now, that is how it was.

Now when we look at the figures on your graph, we see a decline in the number of IPOs coming to the market. Everybody is concentrating on trading. And trading seems to be the only factor that drives stock exchanges. Why? I believe it is because of regulation. Market structure depends on regulation. The SEC, for example, regulates the markets, incentives and disincentives are created, and the market structure takes shape in this fashion. Today, when you have Reg. NMS,[10] which fosters competition from other trading venues, everybody starts concentrating on trading liquidity and trading volumes. But the impact on capital formation and listed companies is ignored.

It is the same thing with MiFID[11] and the European Union. Using that as an example, the European regulators cherish the idea of common regulation and increased competition in the Europe Union. But it is all just about trading, trading, and more trading. Yes, trading is a part of the function of a

[10] Reg. NMS became effective on August 29, 2005. Regulation National Market System (NMS) was approved by the Securities and Exchange Commission in 2005 and introduced two years later to further advance the ideas of a national market system. The regulation includes the order protection, or trade-through rule; access rule (fair access) to market data including quotations; rules on sub-penny trading and on market data specifically. See, http://www.sec.gov/rules/final/34-51808.pdf

[11] The Markets in Financial Instruments Directive, or MiFID, was officially enacted on November 1, 2007. The goal is to integrate the European Union's financial markets and to increase the amount of cross-border investment orders. See, http://www.sec.gov/about/laws/wallstreetreform-cpa.pdf

stock exchange, trading is the complementary function of a stock exchange. But there are many other functions of a stock exchange. And when markets concentrate on trading we get a very blurry vision of markets.

For example, who does the trading in the U.S? Does internalization count? Broker dealers can actually be a part of a transaction, and it is the same in the E.U. An order execution is confused with a transaction. Order execution is the job of a broker dealer. They can slice and dice and do so many things, and maybe flip over and actually get that order executed in the best way possible. The stock exchanges, on the other hand, are responsible for the venue, for the whole infrastructure that provides a platform for multilateral routing and order collection. And that provides a best price discovery mechanism.

The two are somewhat confused right now. The broker dealers are, in effect, doing what exchanges once did. And, as I have noted, regulation affects market structure. So let's talk to the regulators, let's open up their eyes. Not only just the regulators, but the policy makers as well.

WEILD: So regulators are causing some of the problems I have described?

ERKAN: I believe so, yes.

WEILD: A self-inflicted gunshot wound! Greg, you lived in London for several years when you were with Merrill Lynch. What is the view of the Europeans right now towards U.S. capital markets? Some of the regulators are fond of saying that our equities markets are the envy of the rest of the world. Is that true? And, if not, what aspects of U.S. markets are causing concern?

GREGORY WRIGHT: It certainly would have been true 10 years ago. Because that's when the highest aspiration any global issuer was to become a public company in the U.S. It is certainly not true anymore. Today, most entities consider their home market before they list on a global market. When they do list on a global market, they first consider the global markets in Asia or in London.

WEILD: Why? Is it strictly a better cost of capital to access Asian or London markets? Is it an aftermarket support issue in U.S. markets? Is it a higher cost to going public in the Unites States? Is it because their markets are better while ours have arguably declined?

WRIGHT: It is very much a function of market regulation in the U.S. It is expensive to go public in the U.S. because legal costs, various other fees, including banking spreads, are higher in the U.S. There is simply not the same upward pressure on costs in London.

WEILD: Back in July at the London Stock Exchange, I met with executives, including Tim Linacre, CEO of Panmure Gordon, and Julian

Palfreyman, head of Winterflood Securities, the largest trade execution house in the AIM market.[12] I also met with a group from Hermes, which is the Rolls Royce of pension funds in the U.K. When I asked them whether the U.S. stock markets are the envy of the world, they laughed. And I asked, what is it that you don't like? What do you like? Most of them cited Silicon Valley[13] and the old IPO market structure that supported small-cap IPOs and their ability to birth entire new industries, to sustain U.S. economic leadership and create jobs. It was what helped drive the frontend of U.S. competitiveness in the global economy.

They see that edge increasingly disappearing. And they think the market has become increasingly trading-centric, unable to support the kind of growth we once saw. The group attributes the decline to an over-regulation of companies going public and the low-cost trading model. That model no longer provides small public companies with the support in the public markets they once enjoyed.

WRIGHT: London has principles-based regulation as opposed to the rules-based regulation in the U.S. Principles-based regulation is a huge benefit.[14]

WEILD: And they are currently concerned with the direction of MiFID. The European Commission is interested in harmonizing rules across member nations.

WRIGHT: Yes.

WEILD: And there is no shortage of people right now who are concerned about the inability to reach out to investors and to drive liquidity in the AIM market as well. But it is not quite as robust as it was once perceived to be there for a variety of U.K. regulatory reasons. Here's a question that's a little bit rhetorical: Are small IPOs important to economies and why? Should we be taking more small companies public?

BARRY SILBERT: To answer that, you need to look at the capital formation process for companies. Fifteen years or so ago, the capital formation process started with funding by angel investors. The company would then engage a few rounds of venture capital and then go public, on average in

[12] The AIM market is micro-cap division of the London Stock Exchange and consists of generally smaller capitalization companies. AIM is the acronym for Alternative Investment Market.

[13] Silicon Valley has a history of generating IPOs inspired by an entrepreneurial class of creative and business-savvy, technology professionals.

[14] A principles-based approach provides general guidelines of best practice. This contrasts with a rules-based approach which rigidly defines precise provisions that must be strictly adhered to.

4 to 5 years. That process worked pretty well for a couple of decades. But over the past decade, the number of IPOs have declined significantly. The time it takes to go public has now doubled to roughly 10 years on average. We now have a complete breakdown of the capital formation process. Think about that company I just described in its angel stage of development. That company once raised money when it was valued at less than $50 million. It could raise a few rounds of venture capital, and then go public with a market cap of $150 million to $200 million. Today, the average IPO is well above $500 million in market value. The successful ones are more than a billion dollars in market value. If the small-cap IPO is not going to fill up that capital formation hole, perhaps something else does. What would it be?

WEILD: There were many more small IPOs in past years (Exhibit 6.1). A vibrant small IPO market is critical to the growth of an economy. For example, Bernie Marcus, founder of Home Depot, has said he couldn't bring Home Depot public in today's marketplace if it was still at the same early stage and size as it was in its pre-IPO days. Intel, when it went public in 1971 (Exhibit 6.2) was only an $8 million dollar IPO. Adjusted for inflation that would be $44 million dollars in size today. Again, it's another famously small IPO from a different era that has made an outsized contribution to the U.S. economy.

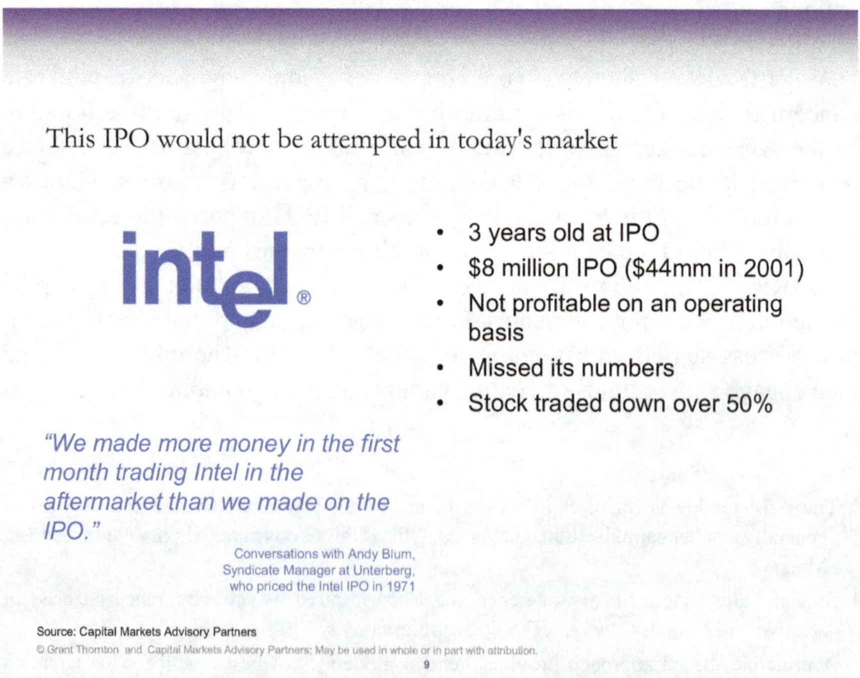

Exhibit 6.2 Intel IPO-1971

Intel was the very picture of risk. Intel missed delivery of their first new product after the IPO and the stock then traded down by 50%. Today, Intel's nano-cap—not even a microcap—float at the time of the IPO would not provide enough economic incentives for brokers to get on the phone and reintroduce the stock to investors when Intel management turned the company around. There wouldn't be adequate economic incentives for research analysts, salesmen, and traders to start calling smaller accounts that could use a nano-cap investment!

Andy Blum, whom some of you may know, was on the board of the NASD and was the equity syndicate manager[15] at Unterberg (the underwriter of the Intel IPO) when the deal was priced. He said that Unterberg made more money trading Intel in the aftermarket than it made on the IPO. If you take a one-size-fits-all trade execution model, and apply the same economic model to micro-cap stocks as you do to large-cap stocks, you will not get good results. The same market structure, applied to both large and small stocks, will create a very different set of outcomes for the two groups of companies. There is certainly an argument for large-cap stocks when it comes to the S&P 500, including stocks like Home Depot, Intel, General Electric and General Motors. The argument is that the best thing to do is just get out of the way and let their buy and sell orders interact. The reason is that these are symmetrical order-book markets that are innately liquid, with lots of buyers and lots of sellers most of the time. In contrast, the natural state of most micro-cap stocks is that their order books are asymmetrical: either big buyer and no sellers, or big seller and no buyers. But somebody has to get paid for liquidity creation. And today there is no effective way to achieve this. Greg, back me up on this. Firms like ThinkEquity[16] can no longer earn a return from liquidity creation in most micro-cap names?

WRIGHT: Everybody who supports micro-cap names—stocks—loses money practically every day.

WEILD: ThinkEquity is smaller in terms of your focus than most folks. I had dinner with Congressman Schweikert[17] recently. Deepak Raj, former

[15] An equity syndicate manager is the professional whose job is to coordinate the marketing and allocation of IPO shares during an Initial Public Offering. The equity syndicate manager will also set the IPO price and oversee all aftermarket price stabilization activities.

[16] ThinkEquity filed for bankruptcy in November of 2012. This bankruptcy, its principals said, was due in large part to the loss of a profitable model to provide liquidity, research and marketing support to small- and micro-cap stocks in the public markets.

[17] Arizona Republican Congressman, David Schweikert, authored key portions of the pro-business Jumpstart Our Business Startups Act (JOBS Act) which passed with bipartisan support in 2012 and was signed into law by the President. See http://schweikert.house.gov/official-biography/

head of equity research at Merrill Lynch, and now on your executive committee, was present and shared how the median equity market value of a company in ThinkEquity's research coverage universe is $1.8 billion.

WRIGHT: Yes, that's the median.

WEILD: $1.8 billion is already four times larger than the median publicly-listed company. If ThinkEquity can't make money at a $1.8 billion median market value, what chance does the median NASDAQ or NYSE-listed company of $450 million dollars in micro-cap market value have of attracting real aftermarket support from Wall Street?.

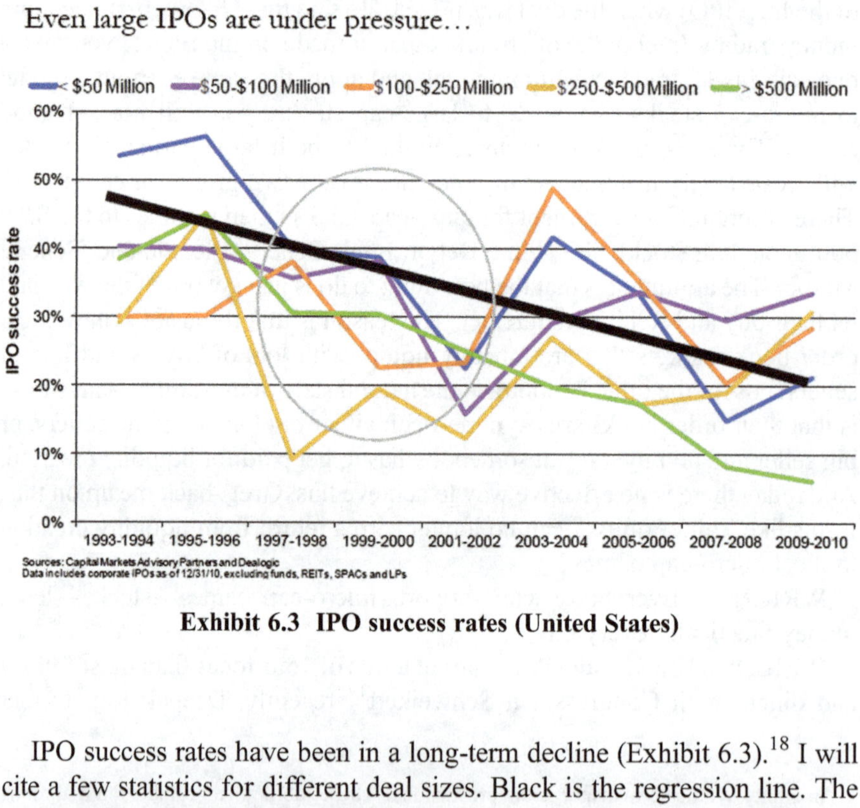

Exhibit 6.3 IPO success rates (United States)

IPO success rates have been in a long-term decline (Exhibit 6.3).[18] I will cite a few statistics for different deal sizes. Black is the regression line. The circle is showing you the period that runs from the implementation of electronic markets in 1997[19] and ending with decimalization in 2001 and,

[18] The speaker defines success here as an IPO that is completed at or within the original IPO filing price range, and is trading at or above the IPO price 30 days after the IPO is completed.

[19] This period of time, a bull market that ran from 1996 to 2000, refers to 1997's Order Handling Rules and 1998's Regulation ATS (Alternative Trading Systems) through the Dot-com Bubble.

finally, Sarbanes-Oxley in 2002. Something isn't right here, as you can see by the decline in IPO success rates occurring during the shift to electronic markets and a bull market. IPOs should have better batting averages during bull markets, not worse. The decline in IPO success rates has been secular and long term in the United States. That may be attributable to a collapse in the distribution and marketing of new issues because of a loss in adequate economic incentives—incentives that support research, sales and capital commitment to sustain newly-public companies. The IPO problem may be an aftermarket market-structure induced problem.

Bob Schwartz said at last year's conference that changes were implemented in market structure in reaction to regulatory changes—and that 10, 15 years later, the markets are still adjusting to those regulatory changes. I remember that Bob specifically cited the Order Handling Rules of 1997, Reg. ATS of 1998 and decimalization of 2001. I was at NASDAQ when decimalization was implemented. It was clear that the number of price points declined as stock quotes were fragmented across one penny increments. However, the depth of the order book declined at each price point so it appeared that liquidity had not changed—at least over the short run. The flaw in the analysis, presented to Congress and the Securities and Exchange Commission at the time, was that it only measured short-term effects. The long-term impact on the broader ecosystem, including the amount of sell-side equity research analyst coverage, capital commitment to support liquidity and equity sales, were not known and could not have been known. But anybody who was present on an equity trading floor 15 years ago versus today, knows that the long-term changes are profound. The trading floors of the 1990s were raucous—traders, sales traders and salesmen were hollering out market information and calling investors. Today's trading floors are eerily quiet.

This is all deals (Exhibit 6.4). You can see the trend line—and again you see IPO success rates continuing to decline both before and after the Tech Crash of 2000.

This is what has happened (Exhibit 6.5). The red line shows the decline in IPO success rates from 1993 to 2010. The orange line shows that median revenues per company spiked pretty dramatically and continued to go up.

As you can see from the next slide (Exhibit 6.6) IPO success rates should have been improving as the quality (revenues) and IPO sizes (liquidity) increased. The exact opposite was occurring. This is evidence of changes to market structure, driven by changes in regulation that are causing a failure in U.S. capital formation, that is to say, IPOs. Investment banks are struggling to put more and more liquidity into the market by requiring bigger and bigger deal sizes—because their institutional clients are requiring it. That's possibly to replace the liquidity being lost as economic incentives are driving market makers out.

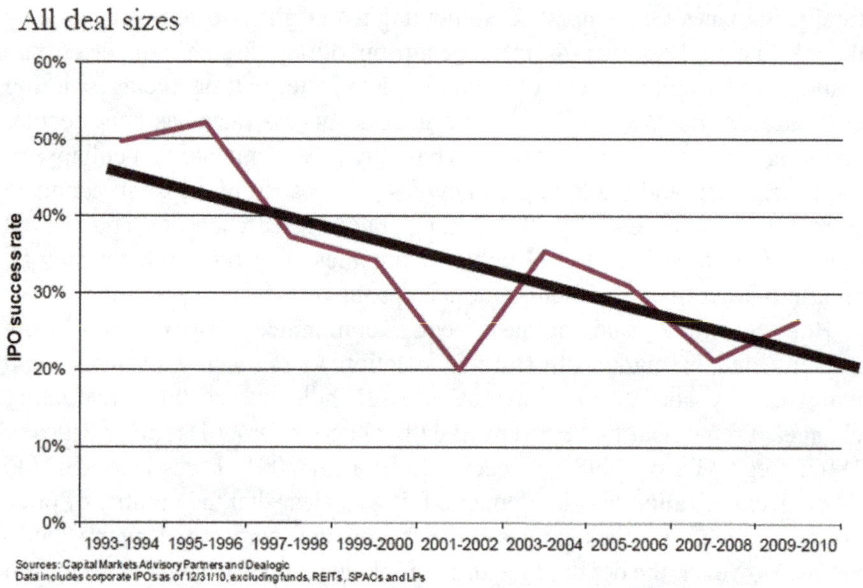

Exhibit 6.4 Overall IPO success rates have been cut in half...

Will markets become so low cost due to competition that thresholds to take companies public will increase so much that the IPO market will become practically non-existent? It seems to be the trajectory. That's unless Congress or the SEC steps in to fix the problem, and brings economic incentives back to a level where small-cap markets function for capital formation, once again.

Joe, you look like you want to be the protagonist here.

JOSEPH HALL: I am probably the only one here who is not an expert on market structure. I am not going to say that this is all because of the Tech Crash. The Tech Crash occurred about 13 years ago. But another thing happened around the time of Reg. ATS and the Order Handling Rules: In 1999, Gramm-Leach-Bliley repealed parts of the Glass-Steagall Act.[20] After that, we had a lot of consolidation in the brokerage industry. Many small

[20] The Gramm-Leach-Bliley Act, also known as the Financial Services Modernization Act of 1999, repealed part of the Depression-era Glass-Steagall Act of 1933. Significantly, it eliminated the barriers among banking, securities and insurance companies that prohibited any one institution from acting as any combination of an investment bank, commercial bank, and insurance company. With the passage, commercial banks, investment banks, securities firms, and insurance companies were allowed to consolidate.

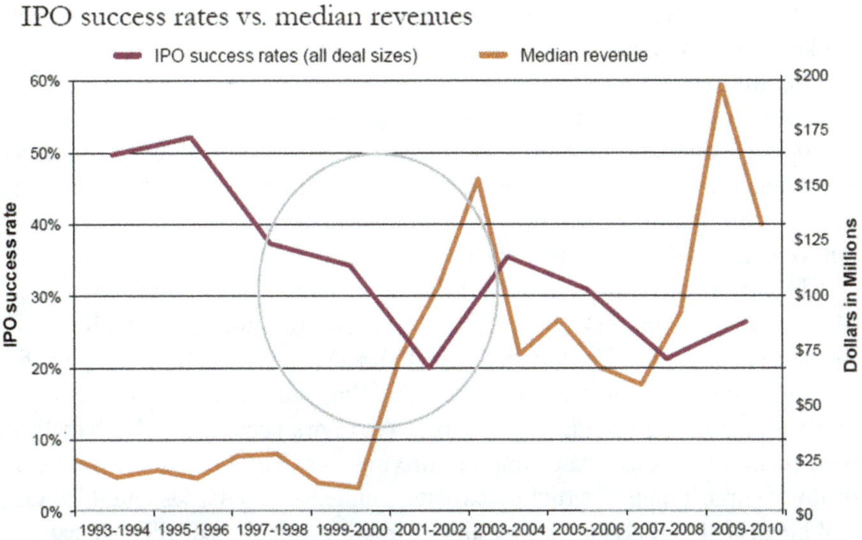

Exhibit 6.5 **. . .even though issuers are more mature. . .**

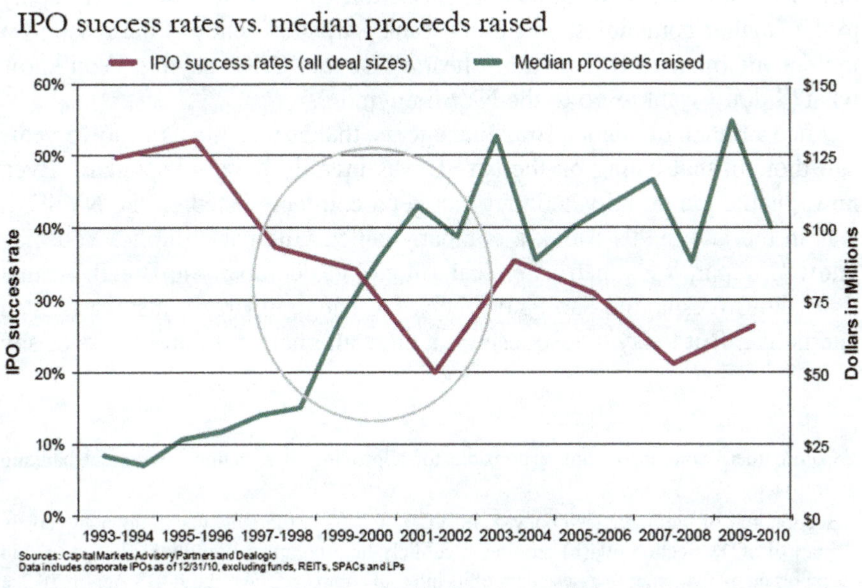

Exhibit 6.6 **. . .and deals are much larger**

broker dealers were purchased by big banks. As a lawyer who deals with bankers and IPO companies, I don't think you can underestimate the impact of commitment committees[21] at the investment banks, and who they are willing to take public. I am not going to mention any of our big clients, but you could probably figure out who they are. If you are one of those very large integrated financial services companies, you might think twice about taking a flyer on an Intel, or some other small company that might (or might not) turn out to be profitable and very innovative in years to come.

Right now, there are a lot of companies coming out of China that would like to access our markets. I think that the equity commitment committees at a lot of the banks are having fits with them. They would love to pick the winners. But they don't want to pick one that will embarrass them with a terrible accounting scandal, or the like. There are secular trends apart from pure market structure issues that are driving this. The investment bankers I deal with aren't market structure experts, neither are the CFOs and the CEOs that I deal with. Nevertheless, we all talk about the decline of IPOs, because it is obviously having a big impact on my business, my firm's business and on what we do. But to tell you the truth, I have never heard somebody say it is the Order Handling Rules or Reg. ATS that killed the IPO market.

You can look at some of these slumps and ask, what does the Tech Crisis have to do with this? Sarbanes-Oxley, which is always so demonized, is only one element to costs. What matters is Section 404.[22] And 404 doesn't apply to the smaller companies, so I don't think Sarbanes-Oxley is the reason for the decline in small IPOs. I don't hear CFOs and CEOs saying, 'You know what? I don't want to go to the NYSE anymore.'

I had a bunch of clients, Brazilian clients, that as recently as 10 to 15 years ago thought that listing on the NYSE was literally the gold standard. Even now, people are proud when they can get a company listed on the NYSE. It was in the late 1990s I took a company called Ultrapar[23] public. You may know Ultrapar, it is a petrochemical, oil and gas company in Brazil. At that time, the Bovespa, the São Paulo Stock Exchange in Brazil, just was not an alternative. But today the Bovespa is a huge alternative. I don't know of any

[21] Commitment committees are responsible for approving or rejecting investment banking transactions.

[22] Section 404 of the Sarbanes-Oxley Act (SOX) of 2002 is the most contentious and costly part of SOX. Section 404(b) requires a publicly-held company's auditor to attest to, and report on, management's assessment of its internal controls. Under the JOBS Act of 2012, a new category of IPOs called Emerging Growth Companies, or EGCs, is allowed to delay implementation (defer cost) of 404(b).

[23] NYSE: UGP.

big Brazilian company that sets their sights now only on the NYSE. They also set their sights on the Bovespa because the Bovespa is a hugely liquid market.

That didn't happen overnight. A lot of buy-side institutions suddenly found Brazil a very attractive place to be. Talking to my friends in Brazil, my impression is they are not saving a lot of money listing on the Bovespa. The Bovespa, if anything, is more intrusive than the NYSE in some respects as a regulator for its listed companies. You can talk to any CFO of a Brazilian company about how many times a day he or she gets a telephone call from somebody at the Bovespa. They are wondering why there is a little bit of strange activity in their stock, ordering them to go out and make a statement, a *fato relevante.*

So, because I am not a market structure guy, it is hard for me to say that Reg. ATS is or is not the reason for this decline in IPOs. There are a lot of factors involved, and to view it all through the lens of market structure, is a bit like a carpenter thinking that everything kind of looks like a nail.

WEILD: It is not Reg. ATS per se. It is the loss of economic incentives for securities firms to make markets in cash equities, whether or not people can make a living supporting companies that need support. Reg. ATS, on the heels of the Order Handling Rules, played a dominant role in the loss of these incentives. That is the first point. About Gramm-Leach-Bliley, you are right.

Let me tell you a story. While I was at Prudential Securities, we had taken a run at acquiring Hambrecht & Quist, years before it was actually sold to JP Morgan. Dan Case, who was president of Hambrecht & Quist, gave me a courtesy call at Prudential before Hambrecht & Quist announced years later that they were selling to JP Morgan.[24] He said the reason they were selling was *not* because of Gramm-Leach-Bliley. He said it was because selling enabled them to diversify away from reliance on the cash equities business. He specifically mentioned that his firm was concerned that the Order Handling Rules were undermining the economics of the cash equities business. The rules would make it impossible to fund the needed overhead to support banking, research, sales and trading during a down– that is, a bear—market cycle.

I believe that it was the loss of economic incentives from the Order Handling Rules and Reg. ATS that precipitated the sale of investment banks—because of how Dan Case explained the rationale for selling Hambrecht & Quist. Graham-Leach-Bliley simply allowed the banks to be

[24] JP Morgan Chase acquired Hambrecht & Quist for $1.46 billion on December 9, 1999.

bidders. Perhaps we'll ask Al Berkeley who is at the conference today.[25] Al was the founder of the tech research and banking practice at Alex. Brown.[26] Alex. Brown was one of the so-called Four Horsemen investment banks that, along with Hambrech & Quist, Robertson Stephens and Montgomery Securities, dominated the tech IPO market for many years. Al actually worked on the Microsoft IPO years ago. Alex. Brown was the co-manager behind Goldman Sachs. Al later became president of NASDAQ. The investment banks were afraid that in a bad equities market, when there was little to no banking business, that they would not be able to keep the lights on.[27]

HALL: The Order Handling Rules cut into the profitability of small broker dealers. But without Gramm-Leach-Bliley there wouldn't be buyers for these investment banks.

WEILD: That's right. They wouldn't have sold the investment banks to the commercial banks. But back up, this is a great point. People are always concerned about this but there is no shortage of firms today that would like to emerge and replace the Four Horsemen.[28] Greg Wright, if ThinkEquity could do it, you would. Am I right?

Looking back now, those were terrific businesses. I know that Tom Weisel, who was running Thomas Weisel Partners, ultimately threw in the towel after the firm got crushed in the wake of the financial crisis and later sold its business to Stifel Nicolaus & Company in 2010. Look at Cowen & Company, another of the likely ones that should have emerged to replace the Four Horsemen. It has had a hard time stepping up to fill that void in the market for small IPOs. Steve Wunsch[29] has thought a lot about these issues.

STEVE WUNSCH: I don't know if you are all aware of the historic milestone we've reached with the topic of today's conference? People

[25] Al (Alfred) Berkeley was President of NASDAQ from 1996 to 2000 and vice chairman from 2000 to 2003. Prior to NASDAQ, Berkeley was a general partner and then a managing director of Alex. Brown & Sons.

[26] Alex. Brown & Sons, the first investment bank in the United States, was founded by Alexander Brown in 1800 and based in Baltimore, Maryland. In 1997, the firm was acquired by Bankers Trust and became part of BT Alex. Brown. In 1999, this was acquired by and absorbed into Deutsche Bank.

[27] Weild, in a follow-up for this chapter, noted that Al Berkeley, who was in the audience during his panel discussion, confirmed this view.

[28] The so-called Four Horsemen were four Wall Street firms that catered to the IPO and growth equity business during the 1970s, 1980s and 1990s. They included Alex. Brown, Hambrecht & Quist, Montgomery Securities and Robertson Stephens.

[29] Wunsch, a well-known market structure commentator, founded the now defunct electronic Arizona Stock Exchange (AZX) in 1990. Prior to AZX, Wunsch was an executive at Kidder Perabody.

attending conferences like this over the last three decades were always 100% concerned with how to reduce the cost of trading. That was basically what all the topics were about, whether you were talking about electronic markets, call markets, continuous market ECNs, ATSs, crossing networks, or whatever. The story of regulation was about whether we can reduce the cost of trading. No one at any of those conferences, on any of those panels, or even in informal conversations that I can recall, ever thought about what it is that enables a stock to be created in the first place. Where do the stocks come from that we are all trading here? This is the first and only conference I can think of in almost three decades of my experience that has actually addressed this topic.

I would like people to consider something that may seem anathema given the history of trying to reduce trading costs. If you consider what incentivizes IPOs, reducing trading costs is not on the list. In fact, reducing trading costs is probably a bad thing. Why? Because people who needed to find the companies to introduce them into their own environments and to their clients—and to profitably trade them—will actually see less incentive to do that. That's if trading costs are forced down by regulation, or by any other means for that matter.

The key here is that, as Hüseyin and others have said, regulation is pushing trading costs down to levels that make what is perhaps the main business of trading stock in the capital markets an unsustainable business. However, while we might like all the features of this low-cost trading market, more is needed. We need to broaden our thinking. You know the old Winston Churchill phrase, 'History is written by the victors.' That thought applies to this topic. Everyone who is still in the business—the winners, at least for now—will basically, in some way or other, be speaking well of the electronic trading models that the SEC has forced upon the markets.

But we should think twice about our expressed certainty that we were doing the right thing all those years—when we were encouraging the regulators to introduce rules designed to force the cost of trading down. Look back at what the NASDAQ dealer market once was. Today we haven't really talked about the NASDAQ dealer market. We have talked about the NASDAQ stock exchange, the NYSE and all the other exchanges. But the NASDAQ dealer market was once called the eighth wonder of the world by Chinese President Jiang Zemin. NASDAQ was where new companies came to the market. The key features of the NASDAQ dealer market were investment banking practices like laddering or spinning that are now illegal. Things that the SEC now clearly bans.

Laddering was when, as a condition of an IPO allocation to an institution, you would encourage the institution not only to flip that stock, but actually to buy more of it after it became public. Spinning was the practice of giving stock allocations to people who might be future investment banking clients.

You would get an allocation at Credit Suisse back in the 90s, if you were one of the so-called Friends of Frank, or clients of Credit Suisse First Boston. That was Frank Quattrone who ran the firm's technology banking unit and reputedly could get you some nice stock in a very profitable IPO.[30]

These are examples of practices that naturally grew up in the NASDAQ dealer market. The practices were very detailed. I would call the environment within which they operated a reciprocity-based social network. And within this all of the participants knew they had an obligation to uphold their practices and the benefits the environment bestowed. Laddering and spinning were examples of it. And to take some of the most outrageous examples from the SEC standpoint, the environment also meant having research conducted by people who were also associated with investment banking, and upholding the quarter tick—the 25 cent spread—prior to the introduction of decimal pricing in the equities markets. In other words, we should question our condemnation of the practice of avoiding those infamous odd eights that Christie and Shultz[31] showed as evidence to the world that NASDAQ market makers were reportedly once engaged in price fixing.

Without taking moral positions on the rights or wrongs of these matters, I urge that it would be wise for all of us to step back and stop focusing myopically on how to reduce the cost of trading. Instead, we should be looking at what it takes to make a community develop the will to be a successful capital formation community. You can see that there are many practices that have been banned by the SEC over the years.

Dave, your charts show a number of other regulatory events that are milestones. Milestones that appear to be associated with, and which perhaps have caused, the decline in IPOs. But even the most outrageous practices you can see were obviously integral parts of NASDAQ's reciprocity-based ethical social networked dealer market. At the end of the day, it was the NASDAQ market that produced the results which everyone had once envied us for. To a degree, not just the SEC, but all of us who participated in all those conferences over the decades, thought we were doing good by eliminating those practices—and all of the trading cost that went along with them. Perhaps we should stand back and think twice about what we have done.

[30] See, Quattrone gets 18 months in prison. Former star banker also gets 18 months for obstructing justice and witness tampering. Krysten Crawford, *CNN/Money.* September 8, 2004. http://money.cnn.com/2004/09/08/news/newsmakers/quattrone/

[31] See, Why Did Nasdaq Market Makers Stop Avoiding Odd Eight Quotes. *The Journal of Finance,* December 1994. William G. Christie; Jeffrey H Harris; Paul H. Shultz. http://www.acsu.buffalo.edu/~keechung/TEM/Journal%20Articles/Collusion%20B%201994.pdf

WEILD: One other major change to market structure that we need to discuss: Reg National Market System (NMS). While it may appear to have fostered competition and led to a proliferation in choice for investors—there are now over 1,000 order types, for example—it actually deprived issuers of the only real choice they had in market structure. Issuers previously had a real choice in the U.S., between dealer markets and specialist markets. By homogenizing everything and throwing 60 different venues into competition with each other, this very meaningful choice for issuers was taken away. The people who suffered the most were the job creators—the issuers.

Here we see the total number of IPOs dating back to 1991 (Exhibit 6.7). The circle shows the Dot-com Bubble[32] period that ran from 1996 to 2000. It surprises most people that the United States was doing 500 IPOs per year on average in the 5 years before the Dot-com Bubble. A common misconception is that the number of IPOs was not elevated during the Dot-com Bubble.

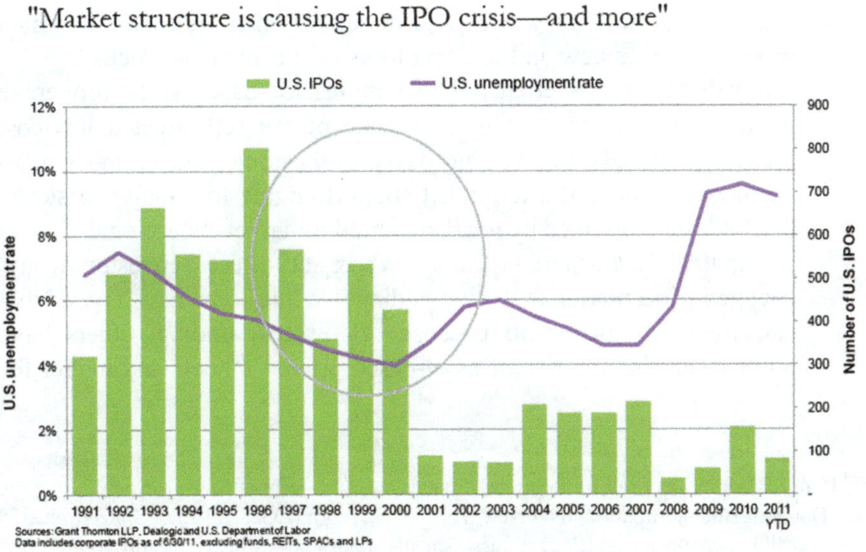

Exhibit 6.7 Market structure adding to unemployment?

[32] The speculative trading bubble (that ultimately burst) spurred by advances in technology and the Internet, the frenzy was characterized by the creation of Internet-based companies that went public. At its peak on March 10, 2000, NASDAQ reached 5,408.60.

But the amount of proceeds was roughly three times the historical level. And it was all concentrated in a very narrow swath of Internet-related industries. This led to a colossal misallocation of capital.

Other data, notably that of Professor Jay Ritter of the University of Florida, shows a significantly higher numbers of IPOs in the 1980s than in the post-dot-com bubble—around 350 on average per year versus the 165 IPOs per year in the post-Dot-com Bubble period. We conclude:

1. The Dot-com Bubble was likely driven by massive asset shifts by retail investors from traditional Wall Street broker-intermediated models into low-cost self-directed brokerage accounts—without brokers acting as buffers to temper speculative excess. Brokers are required to monitor and apply "suitability standards" which usually requires diversification—an inhibitor of speculative excess not found in the self-directed model. Contrary to popular wisdom, the Dot-com Bubble was not caused by Wall Street or a few renegade analysts like Henry Blodget of Jack Grubman.[33] It was caused by the emergence of the Internet that enabled the rapid growth of self-directed brokerage accounts which gave consumers new and exciting tools to speculate on stocks.
2. As Wall Street converted out of commission-based stock brokerage models—in reaction to the emergence of the self-directed low-cost brokerage model—to charging based on customer assets under management, the natural aftermarket support engine for small-cap stocks that had been provided by retail and middle-market institutional brokers was gutted. That ushered in an age where self-directed investors would engage in speculation and "day trading." While some have argued that consumers are better off because of low-cost trading, others have pointed out that the rise of asset-based pricing models and higher fee

[33] Henry Blodget was head of the global Internet research team at Merrill Lynch during the Dot-com Bubble. In 2002, then New York State Attorney General Eliot Spitzer released Merrill Lynch e-mails on Blodget's assessments about stocks which allegedly contradicted what was previously published by Blodget. In 2003, Blodget was charged with civil securities fraud by the Securities and Exchange Commission. He agreed to a permanent ban from the industry, paid a $2 million fine and a $2 million disgorgement.
Jack Grubman, a former managing director of Salomon Smith Barney, he was the lead research analyst for the firm's telecommunications sector coverage. The commission charged that from 1999 to 2001, Grubman issued research reports that concealed material facts and which misled investors. In 1999, he famously upgraded his opinion of AT&T from "neutral" to "buy," according to reports. In a later e-mail, Grubman supposedly explained the change as part of a strategy to have his twin daughters and son accepted into the prestigious 92nd Street YM-YWHA's preschool program. In April, 2003, the SEC banned Grubman for life from the financial industry.

hedge fund pricing represents a form of fee "whack-a-mole."[34] Consumers may be worse off when the impact on the economy of lower capital formation rates is factored in.

3. As the U.S. economy grew in the period preceding the credit crisis, the U.S. should have been producing as many as 900 IPOs a year. Yet we only produced an average of 165 IPOs, never making it back to what had been the levels of even the 1970s.

I lose my patience at times when people refuse to acknowledge the harm these changes in market structure did to our economy, and especially to the small IPO which once represented 80% of all IPOs—and now represents less than 20% of all IPOs. The shift occurring was coincident with Reg. ATS in 1998 and before Sarbanes-Oxley in 2002. We now have a one-size-fits-all stock market structure that may work for large-cap issuers—although that too could be debated. But it is clearly an epic failure for small-cap, micro-cap and nano-cap companies. The loss in economic incentives brought about by this electronic penny-tick size market structure has been quietly killing the entire ecosystem—small investment banks, brokers, research, and capital commitment to support liquidity—in the United States that is required to support the job creators. The small IPO was traditionally the bridge into the public markets. If you can't bring companies public, and there is no access to low-cost public capital, then private company investors will become increasingly risk averse and avoid investing in private companies—especially capital intensive ones that lack well-recognized brands. Look at the venture industry today. You will see there is more and more capital invested in Web 2.0, yet less and less capital invested in industries like biotechnology and hardware, including semiconductors and semiconductor capital equipment. These industries are important to our national security. I always have to look at my friend Al Berkeley in the front row to make sure that he is in agreement with me. Because he knows this stuff cold.

So, here is the listings data in the U.S. (Exhibit 6.8). I don't know how anybody could not be disturbed by this. There has been a 45% decline in the U.S. population of listed companies since the peak in 1997—a steady downward trend! The U.S. is at the bottom—the worst performance—of a list of countries for whom we could obtain reliable data. We stripped monthly reporting data out of the World Federation of Exchanges, scrubbed and complied it, going back to 1991. As you can see, Asia is way outperforming the U.S. Frankly, one of the concerns in London is that the U.K. performance

[34] The term "whack-a-mole" is used colloquially to describe the repetitive and ultimately futile task of "whacking" an adversary that, despite the successive attempts, simply pops up somewhere else each time.

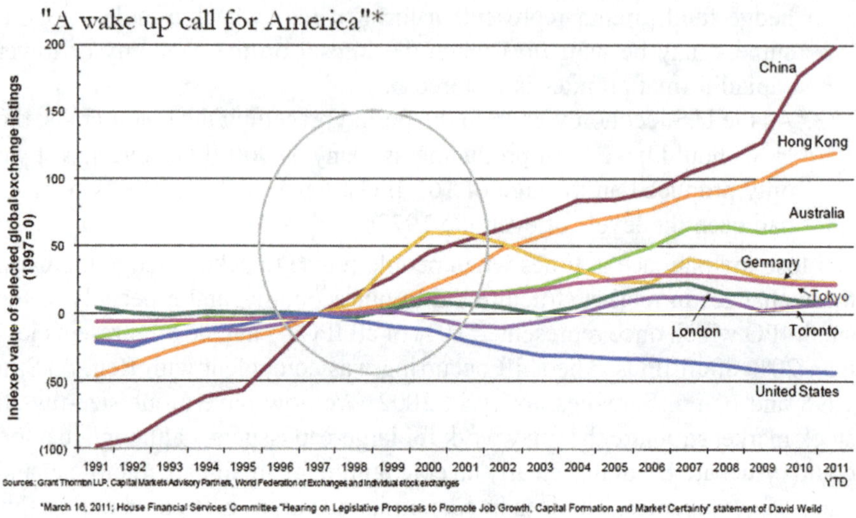

Exhibit 6.8 Decline in listed companies (45%) adding to unemployment?

may be worse than meets the eye. Because the AIM Market in London was started after 2000 and should be helping to fill in the listings numbers in the U.K. with smaller companies. However, if you actually look at the Major Market numbers—that's the segment of larger companies on the London Stock Exchange—the Major Markets is under siege right now and in decline. Notably, the Major Market on the LSE is also an electronic order book market. So it is pretty clear that electronic order books and hyper-efficient penny spread markets, or sub-penny spread markets when applied to smaller companies, is an unmitigated disaster for economic growth.

SEC Mission

"The mission of the U.S. Securities and Exchange Commission is to protect investors, maintain fair, orderly, and efficient markets, and facilitate capital formation." (Source: SEC Website)

Let me ask a rhetorical question: How well is the SEC succeeding in its mission? The mission of the U.S. Securities and Exchange Commission is to protect investors, to maintain fair, orderly, and efficient markets, and to facilitate capital formation. My assessment is that the Division of Corporation Finance at the agency has improved access to capital for already public companies. For example, the use of Form S-3 shelf registrations has created better ways to access capital. For this, the SEC probably deserves an A. But because of problems created mostly by its Division of Trading and Markets—problems that involve market structure—the SEC deserves an F. The small IPO market and model to support smaller public companies has been decimated. Most notably, this is exactly the part of the market that once made the United States the so-called envy of stock markets across the globe. That's a common claim of U.S. regulators and legislators which is now soundly rejected by most people I meet in the international stock exchange and investment communities. Now this is going to stir it up a little bit (Exhibit 6.9). Read the quotes!

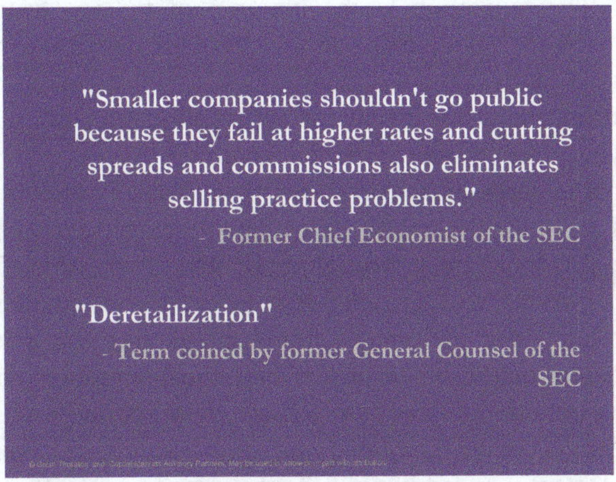

Exhibit 6.9 Quotes

I was speaking on a panel for *Institutional Investor* magazine. The conference was for buy-side traders on the West Coast about six months ago. I asked these buy-side traders, 'What's happened to liquidity in large cap stocks?' Has it improved over the last ten years? And most of them raised their hand to say that liquidity in large-cap stocks had improved. Then I asked, what has happened to the small-cap stocks? These are professionals who mostly represent long-only institutional money managers. The overwhelming majority felt that small-cap liquidity had declined because of the electronic order book markets. This was a fascinating disclosure. By the way, most institutions define small caps as sub-$2 billion dollars in market value. Micro-cap is sub-$500 million in market value.

You can imagine what is happening to nano-cap stocks which are below a $100 million market value. Larry Harris, a former chief economist at the Securities and Exchange Commission who was also on my panel, said to me, 'Smaller companies shouldn't go public because they fail at higher rates, and cutting spreads and commissions also eliminates selling practice problems.' His thesis was that it was a good thing that the SEC took away the incentive to market stock—so you have zero-cost trading markets, hyper-efficient markets, no commissions, and nobody on the phone to sell anything. That's perfect in Larry's estimation because, 'It eliminates selling practice abuses.' My counter was that while it might seem like a great benefit for the consumer, they don't have to pay anything. In fact, we are throwing consumers out of work left, right and center by making it harder for companies to access the growth capital required to create jobs.

Deretailization is a term coined by former SEC general counsel, Brian Cartwright.[35] Deretailization is the notion that we are institutionalizing markets from 144A[36] and, increasingly, through derivative products like exchange-traded funds. We are increasingly taking the single stock selection out of the market, and that is happening across all marketplaces. I urge you to read up on what Brian means by deretailization.

Nothing particularly nefarious about this. Brian is an observer of the markets, and he looks back to some of his speeches he presented while at the SEC. He also looks back through retail stock ownership. Decades ago, something like 80–90% of households were owners of single stocks. Now that has been converted into mutual funds and exchange-traded funds. And now other types of markets have grown up in the institutional marketplace—and these have cut out the retail side. Retail obviously doesn't have the same liquidity constraints in the micro-cap space that institutions have. At one time they very importantly added liquidity to the micro-cap stocks.

Under the theme of deretailization, do you think Barry that we can create a real alternative in the private marketplace to pick up the slack where the public markets have clearly failed with regard to capital formation?

[35] See, The Future of Securities Regulation, Brian G. Carwright, General Counsel, U.S. Securities and Exchange Commission, University of Pennsylvannia Law School for Law and Economics, Philadelphia, Pennsylvannia, October 24, 2007 http://www.sec.gov/news/speech/2007/spch102407bgc.htm

[36] Rule 144A relates to the private resale of restricted securities to qualified institutional buyers for minimum $500,000 units granted a safe harbor from registration requirements.

What needs to occur in terms of regulatory relief? We have a couple of bills in Congress right now that kind of open that up, but can they really do the heavy lifting for the U.S. economy?

SILBERT: Absolutely, and it is happening. You know I get to wear the hat today as both the CEO of an exchange—SecondMarket—and also as an entrepreneur. I can tell you that I don't know one entrepreneur who wants to go public. It is no longer the pinnacle of success. This has been ten years in the making. Do you know what they say to me? Give us an acceptable alternative to the IPO, and we will take that route—even if it that puts our company at a theoretical discount to what the public market may value our company. Regarding Dave's point, when we look at the median market-cap values, there are thousands of these zombie public companies that don't actively trade. Consequently, they get none of the benefits of being a public company. Yet they have all of the negatives of being a public company.

Here is a brief history of how this came about. SecondMarket[37] had been in business a few years when, back in 2007, we were approached by a former employee of Facebook. This gentleman had just left the company, and he had some options that were about to vest and had to exercise them. He said, 'You are a marketplace for other illiquid assets so, can you help me get some liquidity?' And we replied, 'Yeah, you know that Facebook is an exciting company, so let's see if we can be helpful.'

To our surprise, there were a lot of institutions willing to buy Facebook stock which was underlying the options. This was in early 2008. We did some transactions. Before we knew it, we had a lot of interest from buyers and sellers in Facebook stock. Then we said, look let's take a step back, let's figure out what's happening here. That was probably around the time I met Dave [Weild]. I really should commend him for everything he is doing to help solve this problem.

We realized that these companies didn't want to fit into the traditional public market model. We realized that we had an incredible opportunity here, that we had a blank slate to work with. We are able to look at hundreds of years of marketplace development, and to think about where we are at from a technology perspective. I don't mean from a high-frequency perspective, I mean where we are at from the perspective of crowdsourcing and social networks. There are all these powerful tools that we have that are not yet incorporated into the market.

How do we build a better market? What we have done over the past couple of years is build a marketplace where our customer is, in effect, the driver of the company. The company essentially creates a customized market structure

[37] See, SecondMarket website, http://www.secondmarket.com

that is best for them. Instead of forcing a company to conform to what the public market rules require of them, we allow a private company to set the rules around when, for instance, the market for their stock is open.

I mean, God forbid, the company's stock is not trading every millisecond. Most companies want to have trading in their stock at least once a year, twice a year, maybe quarterly. Companies sometimes want to limit who the buyers are within their market. Companies want to put limits on how much stock an employee can sell. Yes, we are regulated, we require companies to put information into our secure system. This includes audited financials and risk factors. But the information we require does not extend to the likes of a Form 10K or Form 10Q, as required by the Securities and Exchange Commission for publicly-registered companies. Our marketplace is for sophisticated, accredited investors, who know the rules, and who enter this market realizing they will not get the same level of information they will find in the public market. They are okay with that. *Caveat emptor*—'buyer beware'—applies.

We have seen an incredible explosion of interest in our market the last couple of years. In 2008, we traded in one stock, Facebook, for about $30 to $40 million in volume. In 2009 we traded a dozen companies for about $100 million. Last year we traded about 40 companies for about $400 million. This upward trend is increasing at a faster and faster rate. What's happening now is the 'network effect.'[38] We have the ability now to expose to our 80,000 investors on our system, companies that they have never had access to before. We can give them the opportunity to invest in these companies before they go public, and the companies are getting liquidity in the process of this same exposure. They are also getting what I think are fair valuations, and they now have an alternative to going public.

They can either grow to the point where they can actually go public and become a billion dollar company or, they can stay private for a few more years until they want to sell themselves.

I have spent a lot of time in Washington, DC. I have been asked to testify in Congress several times. The last time was a couple of weeks ago. As discussed and alluded to earlier on this panel, there are bills in Congress addressing the IPO market and pro-IPO restrictions. They are being accelerated through the U.S. House of Representatives.[39] It is exciting that both the

[38] The effect one consumer of a good or service has on the value of that product to other consumers. A good example is the telephone. The more people who own telephones, the more valuable the telephone is to each owner.

[39] The various bills described by Barry Silbert were ultimately folded into the JOBS Act in 2012.

legislators as well the regulators realize that public market issues have to be addressed. But it is also exciting that we also have to make the private market more efficient. And there is a draft bill that is about to be dropped.

WEILD: What is the draft bill?

SILBERT: It is the General Solicitation bill.[40] In all, there is the bill that has either been dropped (submitted for consideration), or is in draft form, that will allow for a crowdfunding exemption. So that would mean small private companies can raise dollar amounts in small increments from the public. There is a bill to increase the number of shareholders a private company can have before they must be publicly registered with the SEC. Currently, if you have 499 shareholders, you have to file to become a publically-traded company. There is a bill that will increase that number to 2,000. There is a bill that would increase the requirements before a company is subject to Sarbanes-Oxley, meaning companies below a certain size that are going public will be able defer compliance. There is a bill to ban general solicitation so that companies and issuers can talk publically about their private placements. Then there is Reg. A.

WEILD: Reg. A is a very infrequently used exemption from having to file a registration statement with the Securities and Exchange Commission. Historically, a private company could sell up to $5 million in unregistered securities to public investors. But because the offering was subject to state review, or the Blue Sky law, it was seldom ever used when companies could raise an unlimited amount of capital from accredited investors under Reg. D.[41] The bill, HR 1070, proposes to take the Reg. A cap up from $5 million to $50 million. And there is some debate about whether there should be some simplified form of public registration, or NASDAQ and New York Stock Exchange listing, to keep these offerings from being subjected to the state by state review process. All these proposed changes have to go through committees, and to be negotiated. There are some parallel bills in the Senate. And while it may take time, the good news is that Congress seems to be paying attention. If you listened to the Presidents job speech back on September 8th of this year, he mentioned how the Administration wanted to eliminate red tape and make it easier for companies to go public. There is

[40] When the JOBS Act was later signed into law on April 5, 2012, it included as Title II this earlier bill that repealed the prohibition against general solicitation (marketing) of private placements. This gave birth by late 2013 to a new type of Crowdfunding Portal that would offer securities under 506(c) to accredited investors.

[41] Regulation on general solicitation of private security offerings. See, A Trillion Dollar Source Of New Funding? The SEC's New 'Reg. D'. July 13, 2013, Cheryl Connor, *Forbes,* http://www.forbes.com/sites/cherylsnappconner/2013/07/13/a-trillion-dollar-source-of-new-funding-the-secs-new-reg-d/

an increasing awareness of the critical issues. U.S. Treasury Secretary, Timothy Geithner, held a conference on capital formation recently. Some of these panelists here and myself were invited.

If you want to do your respective countries a service, insist that people stop using data from large-cap stocks to impute the experience of investors and issuers in the markets overall. Small-cap stocks are a world apart. We must insist on data and analysis from small-cap, micro-cap and even nano-cap stocks. Don't let people just share data only on large-cap liquidity, and don't let them use volume as a proxy for liquidity because volume is not liquidity. Liquidity has to encompass some notion of price and time. A lot of the comment letters submitted to the SEC in this regard are really misleading They focus exclusively on S&P 500 liquidity or volume, and ignore what happens with the Russell 2000 sector and below.

The Russell 2000 is for small caps. But small cap is not a micro-cap—and over 50% of listed companies in the U.S. are microcap (sub-$500 million) in size or smaller. So we need attendees here today to come up with data measures that look at the health over time, of micro-cap stocks. We need issuers, stock exchanges, and ultimately regulators, to focus on the fate of the microcap market place. And they should do this from the perspective of institutional investors.

I am opening this up to a Q&A.

STEPHEN SAX: [Compliance Officer for FBN Securities]: I found your commentary refreshing concerning the IPO market's effect on unemployment because you know the facts. Today, the exchanges are still listing, but the question is, what are they listing? These derivatives, and these ETFs. I don't know if there is any value to these ETFs from an employment point of view? Are they helping real companies finance their business?

WEILD: There has been discussion that addresses that issue. Harold Bradley[42] published a paper on ETFs. There is concern that the ETFs under weigh the microcap names. And, in so doing, that deprives the microcap stocks of investment that could raise valuations. When does the ETF part of the market become so large that capital formation can't function any longer? Very few of the ETFs actually have anybody home to make an investment decision and to follow up on an equity offering. To the best of my knowledge, none of them invest in IPOs.

If the market became one big exchange-traded fund, there would be zero capital available to invest in IPOs. At some point, you reach a tipping point

[42] Harold Bradley is a well-regarded industry commentator, a former buy-side executive at American Century, who has been outspoken on various market structure practices through the years.

where no capital formation can occur. It is a very real threat. People in the exchange businesses may not want to hear this: One of the concerns is that the shift from member-owned stock exchanges to shareholder-based public stock exchanges, with the presence of many ATS and ECN competitors, may have caused the listed stock exchanges to lose their ability to protect the interests of listed companies. NASDAQ went public on my watch. I was part of its senior management team. And so I have blood on my hands in this respect! We hadn't really anticipated that, when you have to drive earnings per share, you have to go for the large revenue opportunities, for companies that have already achieved critical mass. That means focusing on large caps, and also on mergers with other stock exchanges and trading venues to strip out costs while the firm attempts to get bigger and bigger. It also means focusing on proliferating synthetics including derivative products and ETFs, which can drive stock exchange profitability. It could be true that this for-profit stock exchange model may be incompatible with the mission of serving the economy. Stock exchanges are no longer forceful advocates for structures and regulations that support capital formation for small business.

KAY BREAKSTONE [Breakstone Group]: Since market structure and regulation have had an impact on small-cap companies going public, what kind of an impact has it had on international companies coming to the U.S. doing IPOs and listing here?

ERKAN: The impact is the same. Why should an international company come to the U.S. and make a public offering when an American company is not willing to go public in the U.S.? Why should they when the broker dealers or investment banks are not putting in a sufficient effort to bring companies to market here in the U.S.? The foreign companies go elsewhere. They go to Hong Kong, to China, or to Brazil, for example, and to other places worldwide where the capital formation is still occurring. For one thing, they are coming to Turkey. It really is a matter of many different things.

I want to add one more reason why the number of public offerings are in decline in European markets and in the United States. The exchanges are becoming public and are being traded on their own exchanges. The shareholders in the exchanges are looking at the bottom line. Exchanges no longer can afford to go out and find companies to pitch about the benefits of public offerings, the financial markets and things like that. They normally leave that to the broker dealers. But the broker dealers are doing the same thing. Everyone is competing on trading volume; nobody is actually looking at the listings. As mentioned already, a one and half billion dollars-size company on average is the only type that is profitable to a broker dealer today. How can you actually find many companies of that size?

For the time being, we are enjoying the benefits of being a non-public company at the Istanbul Stock Exchange. And we do have the resources to approach companies about IPOs. We have meetings all over the country. We visit with the Chambers of Commerce in Istanbul. In fact, we talk to thousands and thousands of companies. We pay attention to increasing public awareness. We recognize that companies know about financial markets, but do they really understand what it is that brings them value?

When you present figures, just as you just did David, you can see what a firm like Intel was worth at the time of its IPO, and what it is worth now. You put out those kind of figures and it show others that success can actually be achieved. When the other companies look at this type of data, this sets them on the road to being convinced and persuaded about an IPO. We visit the companies and talk about a public offering. We talk about a sustainability issue for a company. We talk about social responsibility for companies going public. That is also an important part of increasing awareness.

JOE ROSEN [RKA, Inc.]: David, are you suggesting that, if it is possible to turn the clock back so that these exchanges are no longer publically traded—if they become more like a utility, again—this will better provide a public good?

WEILD: There are a lot of things you can do. Right now, we are fiddling while Rome is burning. We have to put Americans back to work, we need to put the global economy back to work. I belong to the International Stock Exchange Executives Emeriti (ISEEE)[43] run by Don Calvin, the former executive vice president of the NYSE. The organization includes professionals from across the globe. When I talked to them about this for the first time, about two years ago, everybody in the international exchange community looked at me and said, 'Oh my God, we are doing the same thing to our markets overseas.'

We have taken our brilliant market structure which is anathema to primary capital formation, and we've spread it like the plague—because it is carried by all of our bulge-bracket firms, by all of our clients and institutions. They want it so that, increasingly, there is some harmonization across world markets. And I would say that this disease is being spread broadly and globally.

Perhaps we need to have our cake and eat it too. On the one hand, it was never a good thing to charge people too much money to execute an Intel

[43] ISEEE is a global non-profit organization of current and former senior executives from stock and derivatives exchanges, educational in nature, and providing a forum for sharing ideas and insights. See background, http://www.sec.gov/info/smallbus/acsec/iseeeorlandodeclaration2012.pdf

trade. On the other hand, we have to support primary capital formation. To have our cake and eat it too, we need to have a more suitable economic model in the business with appropriate incentives for the broker dealers. Here is something I don't think Barry spoke of. In the private markets, you are not subject to the likes of Reg. NMS, the Order Handling Rules.

There are a couple of positive things that can actually be done in public markets. You can start an experimental market that focuses on small caps as its primary mission. With a different rule book, this will drive capital formation in the U.S. Next, you can have two markets for issuers to select. You can give issuers the choice to set their own tick size, whether in decimal or fractional increments. What a change that would make. All of a sudden, Intel could say, I've too much, they are treating my stock like a casino chip. By the same token, we could trade a microcap name with a 20 cents or 25 cents tick. That possibility would force a conversation with long-term investors, and it could totally alter stock boards.

The third thing is to open up the private market so that this market can pick up the slack. As the economy is hurting, while people are looking for jobs, we need to do lots of things. Over the last decade, not having functioning IPO markets has cost the U.S. economy 10 million jobs by some calculations.

SAM BALABON [Deep Liquidity]: As I see it, the market has no ability other than to put transaction costs on a screen and let people know what they are. There is no way to compensate the providers of liquidity for illiquid stocks—until the market provides a means for these liquidity providers to charge sufficiently for their service. Without this, you will have instruments that have no liquidity. And these smaller firms are simply not going to enjoy the benefits that larger-cap, highly- traded companies enjoy because of their size.

WEILD: Do you have an economic model in mind?

BALABON: Our current economic model offers no way to charge for the extra risk incurred when providing liquidity to small-cap stocks. There is no way of taking risk and converting it into a commodity. You have to have participants. There is risk in providing liquidity, and there are no tools for doing so.

ERKAN: There are things that exchanges can do no matter what their structure is. Whether it is profitable or non-profitable, it doesn't matter. It really has to do with innovation. Stock exchanges never look at a primary market operating or maintaining private markets. There are very different alternatives for bringing a company to a stock exchange, or to a central order book where thousands and thousands of people can actually look at a stock and buy at the first auction. You can go through a primary market auction, for example. In Turkey, we have managed to bring in about two thirds of the public offerings this year through a primary market rather than through a book dealer. This brings down the cost of going public. Maybe the cost is one fourth or one fifth of what it would have been if they were book building in large road shows and things like that. It does work. It takes some innovation on the part of the stock exchange—and we have done it.

WEILD: I want to thank the panelists and attendees. You have been terrific.

CHAPTER 7: THE TRANSFORMATION OF AN EXCHANGE

Larry Leibowitz, *NYSE Euronext*

ROBERT SCHWARTZ: I am not taking the Direct Market Access route to Larry Leibowitz. Bill Freund, a highly respected intermediary, will introduce him. Bill and I share a lot in common. We are both academicians. We both know what it is like to organize and indeed to run a conference. For a long time, Bill Freund ran his excellent conference at PACE University in New York City. While he ran his conference in the fall, I ran mine here at Baruch in the spring. And so we divided up the seasons, a bit like how Portugal and Spain had once divided up the globe. For many years before that, Bill was also the Chief Economist at the New York Stock Exchange. It is my great pleasure to introduce my distinguished friend, Bill Freund.

BILL FREUND: I am very pleased to introduce Larry Leibowitz, Chief Operating Officer of the NYSE Euronext. I have nothing but nice things to say about Larry and for a very good reason. My monthly pension check comes from his office [laughter]!

I have worked on staff at the NYSE with many heads of the exchange, starting with Bob Hack. Then along came Mil Batten. I remember when Mil Batten first arrived at the exchange. He had been Chairman at JC Penny. He looked around and said, 'Is this exchange a department store with just one product?'[1] Then along came John Phelan, who was followed by a young man named Dick Grasso. They were all distinguished in their own way. Now, as you know, the CEO today is Duncan Niederauer.[2]

[1] Stock trading.

[2] These served as Presidents of the NYSE: Robert (Bob) Hack, 1967–1972; John Phelan, 1980–1984; Richard (Dick) Grasso, 1988–1995. William (Mil) Batten was Chairman, 1976–1984. At the time of writing, it was announced that Duncan Niederauer, a former Goldman Sachs executive who became CEO of the NYSE in December 2007, would leave the exchange in August 2014, following the earlier acquisition of NYSE Euronext by Atlanta-based. IntercontinentalExchange Group Inc. (ICE). He was succeeded by Thomas

R.A. Schwartz et al. (eds.), *The Economic Function of a Stock Exchange*, Zicklin School of Business Financial Markets Series, DOI 10.1007/978-3-319-10350-1_7

Larry, together with Duncan Niederauer, is a pioneer and innovator with a sharp eye on the future of exchanges. And that, I am proud to say, is the topic of Bob Schwartz's thought-provoking conference today. As you all know, the efforts by the NYSE to merge with the Deutsche Boerse have made newspaper headlines. And if approved, the world of international equities markets will never again be the same.[3] Welcome Larry.

LARRY LEIBOWITZ: Back in 1981 when Bill Freund was Chairman of the New Jersey Council of Economic Advisors,[4] I was just a lowly Princeton graduate engaged in economic research for its staff. I soon realized that I was not cut out for research. That was not due to your leadership, Bill, not at all. As the last speaker today, I will be brief. I am standing between you and an open bar [laughter]. You would be surprised to hear that at the NYSE we agree quite strongly with some of today's discussion. In that light, I would like to tie together some of the themes that we have heard about an exchange in the modern world.

An exchange today is very different than it was in the days of Dick Grasso or any of his predecessors. I am privileged to be affiliated with the largest stock exchange in the world. It is, as you all know, part of NYSE Euronext, which is the world's largest exchange group. Today, the value of stocks listing on NYSE totals about $13 trillion. That is bigger than the next three largest exchanges in the world combined.[5] On the other hand, most people don't even realize that we have a large group of small-cap and mid-cap stocks. In fact, more than 50% of our companies are small-cap and mid-cap stocks.

The traditional role of a stock exchange, of course, is to help companies raise capital by establishing transparency in an efficient secondary market for securities. Companies go public to provide an exit for investors, to obtain currency for mergers and acquisitions, or M&As, and to fuel future growth. It is well known, and as we heard earlier today, that job growth really is fueled by companies in the first couple of years after they have had their IPOs. That is when companies get the capital it takes to expand. As we saw even in the teeth of the economic crisis a couple of years ago, companies like Rosetta

Farley, COO at the NYSE. Leibowitz left the NYSE at the end of 2013 just after the acquisition was completed.

[3] See, NYSE Euronext And Deutsche Boerse Terminate Business Combination Agreement (Press Release, February 02, 2012) http://www.nyse.com/press/1328178461772.html.

[4] New Jersey Council of Economic Advisors reports on the economy to the state government.

[5] Next three after NYSE Euronext are NASDAQ OMX, Tokyo Stock Exchange and London Stock Exchange. See, Top Ten Stock Exchanges in the World by Market Cap in 2011. http://www.world-stock-exchanges.net/top10.html.

Stone and Under Armour were hiring.[6] Meanwhile, everyone else was either frozen out or laying off employees. Exchanges for commodities and other asset classes similarly provide an important mechanism for pricing, risk transfer, and risk management. In this mechanism, suppliers and consumers of financial products are a critical part of the overall financial infrastructure and in the broader task of helping regulators manage systematic risk.

Here's another theme that we saw played out heavily over the last few years. The byproduct of this new secondary market is that investors, both institutions and individuals, have skin in the game. Their investments in companies and in other assets give them a chance to participate in economic growth. Their values rise and fall with business performance. That is how investors accumulate wealth. That is how they plan for retirement. That is how they secure their own well-being. And the so-called wealth effect, through rising markets, drives consumer spending. That, in turns, leads to further growth and investment. When it works as planned, it is a virtuous circle.

The twin functions of helping issuers raise capital and in providing a mechanism for investors to accumulate wealth, are a symbol of a nation's economic success and opportunity. All through history, nations have championed their exchanges and viewed them as their symbol of sovereignty. Indeed, the last couple of exchange mergers were blocked based on nationalistic concerns.[7] As a matter of fact, one of the first things emerging countries do as they develop their economies, is to start up a stock exchange. That's a symbol that they are joining the developing world.

The façade of the NYSE, I remind you, is a registered trademark. But a certain ambiguity has clashed with this great symbol of US financial markets and capitalism to the point where we get people marching past our doors holding placards protesting stuff we don't quite understand. It has nothing to do with us! Still, the NYSE's façade is the symbol!

Today, market activity is covered minute to minute all around the world, with prognosticators, investors, companies and politicians using it as a proxy for their feelings of well-being. We go home at night after a market crash and we sure don't feel so good. As I was coming in today, Bill Freund walked up to me and asked, 'What's going on, we were down 250 yesterday?' In fact, the dramatic market sell off following the US House's failure to pass the

[6] NYSE ticker symbols: RST (Rosetta Stone) and UA (Under Armour).

[7] For a closer look at these nationalistic concerns, the "takeover" of domestic exchanges by foreign rivals, See, London and Toronto Exchanges Call Off Merger, Ian Austen, *New York Times,* June 29, 2011. http://dealbook.nytimes.com/2011/06/29/london-and-toronto-exchanges-call-off-merger/?_php=true&_type=blogs&_r=0#.

original TARP bill, played a big role that helped turn around that vote the very next day.[8] That is the power of the stock market.

A position at center stage is attended by a large dose of responsibility. The average American does not understand how the market functions anymore. The average American does not understand that most retail orders never even make it to an exchange floor. And I can confirm this from first-hand experience, having answered many calls after May 6th from investors asking why did their stocks trade here.[9] In fact, their stocks didn't trade here. They just don't get that.

They don't understand that their orders can be executed in the US at numerous exchanges and dark pools.[10] They don't understand what all the technological changes and hyper competition in the US market means for them. In the last 10 years, we have seen huge decreases in investor costs, whether measured by trade commission, exchange fees, execution quality, or spreads.[11] Yet the average investor has been convinced otherwise. They don't feel it or see it that way. It is our job as exchanges, in conjunction with regulators, to give investors in public companies the confidence that the financial markets are not rigged, that they are not a casino, that they are a place where the little guy gets a fair shake.

The way to do this is through increased transparency and reporting, and through better surveillance and enforcement. In the US, the Securities and Exchange Commission and the Financial Industry Regulatory Association, in cooperation with the exchanges, have embarked on a number of measures designed to improve the situation. These measures include the proposed

[8] A headline in the *New York Times*, September 29, 2008, the day after the House originally rejected this $700 billion rescue package for Wall Street in the Troubled Asset Relief Program (TARP), sums it up: House Rejects Bailout Package, 228-205; Stocks Plunge.

[9] The Flash Crash occurred on May 6, 2010 with the Dow Jones Industrial Average declining about 1000 points, about nine percent, only to recover those "losses" within minutes.

[10] There were 13 public exchanges and up to 50 dark pools in the U.S. as of writing in September 2013. That total number of exchanges could change with the pending merger of Direct Edge and BATS, as announced in August 2013, to form the second largest exchange in the U.S.

[11] This is extensively examined in academic studies and literature. Many critics say current market structure practices are disadvantageous and costly to retail investors. On the opposite side, there are proponents of these same structural changes who view them as beneficial for retail investors. See, for example, The Testimony of Thomas M. Joyce, Chairman and Chief Executive Officer Knight Capital Group, Inc. Submitted before The Committee on Financial Services Subcommittee on Capital Markets and Government Sponsored Enterprises, United States House of Representatives Hearing on Market Structure: Ensuring Orderly, Efficient, Innovative and Competitive Markets for Issuers and Investors. Wednesday, June 20, 2012. http://www.knight.com/newsroom/pdfs/researchCommentary06202012.pdf.

central audit trail, Large Trader Reporting systems, and several other measures [12] We need to get these implemented in a reasonable amount of time and at reasonable cost to allow regulators to effectively surveil complex markets and restore investor confidence.

While competition is a great way to spur innovation and lower cost, we need to avoid having exchanges become a dumping ground where orders get placed only after exhausting all other off-exchange possibilities. The long-term consequences are that it becomes more and more difficult to incent anyone to provide liquidity on an exchange, resulting in increased spread and volatility that damages confidence in the public markets. The irony is, as the previous panel noted, all of this contributes to the decease in status of our exchanges as being centrally important to the financial markets. All the while, the rest of the world's markets are championing theirs.

The market for capital raising has, likewise, become more competitive both in the US and globally. Last year three of the top four exchanges for IPO proceeds were Chinese with the NYSE ranking number two. This year, the NYSE leads the world in capital raised with four times the proceeds of the next competitor. But again, four of the top six exchanges are based in Asia.

Down to their very core, exchange competition for listings has spurred changes in the exchanges themselves. To help win their listings, the NYSE now offers a full range of competitive services to listed companies. When GM emerged from bankruptcy, we had to pitch for that listing.[13] It was competitive. Meanwhile, we have experienced an almost 50% increase in our market share of tech IPOs this year with our increased competitive focus on technology. Ten years ago, who would have dreamed that companies like Pandora and LinkedIn would be calling NYSE their home? [14] Today's transfer of Level 3 to the NYSE upon completion of their Global Crossing merger, just underscores this repositioning as a listings choice for global technology companies.[15] And, just as we have talked about this virtuous circle of companies going public and trading in the secondary market feeding

[12] For more on CAT and Large Trader Reporting, which was approved in 2011. see, Sifma Urges End to Some Data Systems as Audit Trail Nears. Nina Mehta, *Bloomberg,* March 28, 2013 http://www.bloomberg.com/news/2013-03-28/sifma-urges-end-to-some-data-systems-as-audit-trail-approaches.html.

[13] See, General Motors Gains in NYSE Return After IPO Raises $20 Billion. David Welch, Lee Spears & Craig Trudell, *Bloomberg,* November 18, 2010, *http://www.bloomberg.com/news/2010-11-18/general-motors-returns-to-nyse-after-raising-20-billion-in-ipo.html.*

[14] Ticket symbols P (Pandaora) and LNKD (LinkedIn).

[15] See, Level 3 Completes Acquisition of Global Crossing. Press Release, Oct 04, 2011. http://www.prnewswire.com/news-releases/level-3-completes-acquisition-of-global-crossing-131036448.html.

economic growth, exchanges are important advocates for the capital formation process.

When companies face hurdles, whether with excess regulation or with the cost of going public, they make other decisions, as we heard before. They could, for instance, stay private, or sell to a larger company, or list on an alternative location. The long-term implication of this makes one country less attractive as the capital center than another, and ultimately a less attractive place to do business. These considerations will be increasingly important over the next 10 years as we continue to see huge numbers of IPO's coming from developing countries. The math works this way as these economies grow far faster than our economy, and as small and medium size businesses continue to face high hurdles to going public in the United States.[16]

Let me comment on the characterization of market structure today as being two-tiered or bifurcated. It's a market that works great for very large-caps stocks, but that doesn't do so well for small-caps stocks. That's a very accurate characterization. We have a one-size fits all market structure that doesn't completely work. That is just a small piece of the puzzle. The entire capital chain is not working for small and mid-size companies. That applies across the board, whether it is one-size-fits-all corporate governance, Sarbanes-Oxley standards, market structure, investment banking rules, or the research settlement[17] that made it difficult for very small and medium size companies to get research coverage of any economic value.[18]

The NYSE sees its role as being a very strong advocate in this area. I would strongly disagree with the previous panel that said exchanges are not interested in the smaller companies. You can look at my travel schedule. It involves visits to Israel, Brazil, Russia, and elsewhere in America and throughout the world trying to figure out how to get these markets functioning better for every size company. Not everybody can be a $10 billion market-cap company. But even this is too narrow a concept of what it means to be an exchange in today's world.

An exchange is a business community. The companies listed on the NYSE represent 80% of the Fortune 500. Yet half of our companies are small- or

[16] See, The costs of going and being public may surprise you. (PWC, September 2012). http://www.pwc.com/en_us/us/transaction-services/publications/assets/pwc-cost-of-ipo.pdf.

[17] The Sarbanes–Oxley Act of 2002, otherwise known as the Public Company Accounting Reform and Investor Protection Act (Senate) and Corporate and Auditing Accountability and Responsibility Act (House) and more commonly called SOX, is US federal law that established new or enhanced standards for all U.S. public company boards, management and public accounting firms.

[18] See, SEC Fact Sheet on Global Analyst Research Settlements. (April 28, 2003) http://www.sec.gov/news/speech/factsheet.htm.

medium-cap. In keeping with transparency and integrity, our job, on the one hand, is to be an advocate of transparency and of good corporate governance standards. But, at the same time, we must be a conduit of business concerns to policy makers and politicians. As an example, NYSE formed a corporate governance commission which contributed to the debate about standards emerging from Dodd-Franks. We have hosted numerous roundtables on tax reform and job creation. We have taken issuers directly to Washington to express their feelings and to talk about why it is not working. We helped foster much needed dialog between business policy makers in the US and other countries around the world. That is our role.

Exchanges should also be clearing houses for ideas on best practices and corporate responsibility. As an example, there are NYSE forums on Green Grid Computing,[19] entrepreneurship, and that all important topic, financial literacy. Investors know far too little about their own economic circumstances, and the decisions they make on a daily basis that affect their well-being. In pursuing this course, exchanges provide businesses with leadership and information exchange.

The massive transformation in the industry has also meant that exchanges have had to become leading edge innovators in technology. On a busy day, the NYSE processes two billion messages at sub-millisecond latency, over highly secure networks that span the globe. Our clients are facing these exact same challenges. If we are processing two billion messages, so too are they.

At a time when banks and brokers are struggling to rationalize their infrastructure costs, exchanges can be depended upon as a neutral, trusted technology partner. These services help banks and brokers to be more efficient, and to allocate internal resources more effectively. The developed market has become more competitive, while other asset classes such as derivatives have seen enormous growth. Moreover, growth in the developing world has dwarfed that in the US and Europe. And it promises to do so for some time to come.

Exchanges have to evolve to meet new challenges. The capital markets are becoming increasingly interconnected and global, particularly in the derivatives space where capital can flow between venues and geographies with relative ease. At the same time, regulators are increasingly concerned about systemic risk. It is more important than ever that exchange regulation and market regulation be coordinated on a global level.

[19] Government standard for energy efficient and more resourceful data centers and computing. See, NYSE Euronext And Deutsche Boerse Terminate Business Combination Agreement. (Press Release, February 02, 2012) http://www.nyse.com/press/1328178461772.html.

In any event, we feel the NYSE Euronext merger with Deutsche Boerse is an important step in fortifying our position in Europe in the rapidly developing derivatives landscape, and in delivering much needed benefits to our clients through margin relief and cost savings.[20] Furthermore, this is more recognition of the globalization of markets, whether equities, derivatives, commodities, or any other instruments. Today's exchanges are now public, for-profit companies. As a result, they have additional responsibilities to shareholders, and they need to balance a host of other interests as well.

It is easy to say, 'Oh well, they are public companies, that is the problem.' They were member-owned companies before, and back then they served the interest of their members. But even back then they did not necessarily serve the interests of issuers and investors. That problem hasn't changed; it is just different today because the owners of exchanges are public shareholders rather than seat holders, brokers and banks. Our job is to figure out how to balance these often conflicting interests. That, in addition to the increased competitive pressures felt in most markets, have greatly accelerated innovation and change in the exchange space. NYSE Euronext is a classic example of this. NASDAQ went through the same process of change, and so have many other exchanges, which have had to embrace change in order to survive and thrive. Amid all this, we must stay focused on maintaining market transparency and fairness. We must ensure that the capital formation cycle continues. We need integrity and trust in what we do. That is essential for NYSE Euronext, and all the other exchanges. In all of our markets, we must foster participation by investors in a way that, in turn, benefits local, national, and global economies. Doing so will also engender confidence, which flows into other areas such as business and consumer spending. It's our job to keep that virtuous circle alive, even as the ground below us shifts.

I thank everyone for being here. It has been a great conference. I very much enjoyed some of the comments today. I welcome your questions.

(Applause)

JOE ROSEN [RKA Inc.]: You mentioned the numerous exchanges, dark pools, various execution mechanisms, and venues in the US. What is the optimal number for the marketplace at large? Is there anything that can be done to bring that about?

LEIBOWITZ: It is hard to figure out how much competition is too much. The question really is, are all of the players being held to the same standards of regulation and surveillance? Is everyone playing by the same rules? I would certainly submit that, in the current US market structure, the

[20] See, NYSE Euronext And Deutsche Boerse Terminate Business Combination Agreement. (Press Release, February 02, 2012) http://www.nyse.com/press/1328178461772.html.

various barriers to entry are too low and the standards are not uniform. That has been a subject of an SEC Concept Release.[21]

Once, there was an exchange duopoly between the NYSE and NASDAQ. Then the regulators sought to swing the pendulum the other way, to introduce greater market competition.[22] At this stage, it is hard to get that swing to stop. It is time to take a closer look at market structure, and not just say that 60 is the right number of exchanges, or that 40 is the right number, or maybe that it should be 20. What we have to do is to figure out the right amount of regulation, and what the cost barriers are that would make a natural equilibrium in this equation. I think we have lost sight of it.

BOB O'BRIEN [KCI Technologies]: As a public company, can you talk a bit about the research and development that has been going on at the NYSE Euronext, and how it is being funded? What are some of the things on the horizon?

LEIBOWITZ: You know it is always a challenge. Our management team arrived at a time when the NYSE had recently gone public. To be honest, the NYSE wasn't really ready to be a public company. The regulatory barriers had been stripped away, and Reg NMS was implemented overnight.[23] We had just done a couple of big mergers, so we had a lot of wood to chop in terms of cost cutting, in terms of changing the technology to be in the right decade at least, and in terms of getting us to the right place with our market model. All of those things took a lot of effort. We try to work on executing that plan while looking at what we must do strategically to get to the next place.

One of those innovations was our acquiring the American Stock Exchange in order to buy an options venue that we then mutualized.[24] Starting US Liffe

[21] Review of the current equity market structure, See, http://www.sec.gov/rules/concept/2010/34-61358.pdf.

[22] The SEC's introduction of the Order Handling Rules in 1997 had arguably the most far-reaching impact on this "duopoly," opening the market to new competitors. The Order Handling Rules included "Limit Order Display Rule" and the "Quote Rule" and paved the way for a wave of upstart ECNs, or Electronic Communications Networks.

[23] Reg NMS became effective on August 29, 2005. Regulation National Market System (NMS) was approved by the Securities and Exchange Commission in 2005 and introduced 2 years later to further advance the ideas of a national market system. The regulation includes the order protection, or trade through rule; access rule (fair access) to market data including quotations; rules on sub-penny trading and on market data specifically. See, http://www.sec.gov/rules/final/34-51808.pdf.

[24] The NYSE's acquisition of the American Stock Exchange was completed on October 1, 2008. See, http://www.nyse.com/press/1222772889985.html.

as a futures platform in a partnership with NYPC and DTCC was another innovation.[25]

On the technology side, we face huge challenges, just in terms of the quantity of data that we have to process in ever shorter periods of time. Not only is it a low-latency computer exercise, it is also about how do you manage processing this enormous amount of data? You know that we have offered some of it out in the cloud—for example, historical analysis and things like that.[26] But, at the same time, we are looking at data warehousing and fast computing to address our needs and those of our customers. That innovation has to happen at all levels. Some of it is pure technology innovation, some of it is business model innovation, and some of it is asset class innovation. And it is our management job to make smart decisions about where to put our investment dollars. We are doing this while running the rest of our business effectively. All of this needs to be balanced.

In some ways, it is the same challenges that companies face when they look at what they will lose in the long run if they run their business just for quarterly earnings. If you are not making your investments for the long run, sooner or later you will run out of costs to cut. That is particularly so if you do not have pricing power, and the market isn't growing, as the US equities markets really aren't. You end up stagnant!

We must constantly think about the next step ahead, about how we will get to the next place. Since the rest of the global marketplace is clearly growing faster than we are, should we be participating more actively on the global stage? And other asset classes are growing faster than equities in the US. How do we continue to thrive? How do we get more scale in this business which, more and more, is a scale business?

BRETT REDFEARN [JP Morgan]: You mentioned that the one-size-fits-all market structure doesn't work. A lot of people have seen some of the issue from the perspective of small and mid-cap companies. What are your thoughts on rethinking Reg NMS for small mid-cap companies? Is there something we should be thinking about for trading the illiquid securities?

LEIBOWITZ: I am not sure that Reg NMS is the real problem. I think it has more to do with decimalization and being forced to add penny trading

[25] Further underlining the growth in this project, see Press Release, March 14, 2012, LCH. Clearnet, NYPC, DTCC and NYSE Euronext Collaborate to provide unprecedented clearing and margining efficiencies for market participants. http://www.nypclear.com/media-center/press-releases/lchclearnet-nypc-dtcc-and-nyse-euronext-collaborate-provide-unprecedente.

[26] In June 2011, NYSE Euronext rolled out a cloud platform, known as NYSE Technologies Community Platform, in collaboration with EMC and VMW. The idea is to allow trading entities to outsource more of their trading infrastructure to the exchange's data centers.

increments so that the spreads in stocks can be artificially narrow.[27] Today, investors can narrow the spread with very low risk. It completely discourages display of liquidity in stocks that are less liquid.[28] At the very least, I would prefer having wider trading increments in another segment of the market.[29] Whether that is an opt-in, or whether that is based on some trading volume, I don't know.[30] We have actually had ongoing conversations about this with regulators. There is empathy for the problem. Still, it is a pretty big rock to lift, and we can't do it on our own. We are subject to Reg NMS.

[27] As David Weild and Edward Kim have noted: "Consumers and institutional investors undoubtedly benefited from decimalization and $0.01 spreads in the trading of large capitalization stocks whose visibility and broad research coverage outweighed any loss of broker and trader support. Unfortunately, decimalization was "one-size-fits-all" and was applied equally to small capitalization stocks that had comparatively little natural visibility."
See, Market Structure is causing the IPO crisis—and More. David Weild and Edward Kim, Grant Thornton, June 2010. http://www.grantthornton.com/staticfiles/GTCom/Public%20companies%20and%20capital%20markets/Files/IPO%20crisis%20-%20June%202010%20-%20FINAL.pdf.
Getting "Pennied": The Effect of Decimalization on Traders' Willingness to Lean On the Limit Order Book at the New York Stock Exchange. Robert Jennings, June, 2001. http://www.nyse.com/pdfs/pennying1.pdf.

[28] The reference here is to the small-cap sector that Leibowitz and, for that matter, other market critics, argue is hurt by trading in penny increments.
See Update, Exchanges Said to Prepare Pilot Program for Changing Tick Sizes. Sam Marmudu and Dave Michaels June 14, 2013 *Bloomberg*, http://www.bloomberg.com/news/2013-06-14/exchanges-said-to-prepare-pilot-programs-for-changing-tick-sizes.html.
From the *Bloomberg* story:
"US markets moved to pricing in pennies from sixteenths of a dollar in 2001 as part of a law intended to reduce costs for investors. President Barack Obama's Jumpstart Our Business Startups Act of 2012 authorized the SEC to look at the impact of decimalization and set a minimum trading increment of as much as 10 cents for emerging-growth companies, or those with revenue of less than $1 billion a year."
"The SEC and exchanges are working on the pilot as some lawmakers in Congress say smaller public companies should be allowed to select their own tick size. A bill introduced last month by Representative David Schweikert, an Arizona Republican, would allow certain companies to choose increments of either 5 cents or 10 cents."
The bill is called, Tick Size Flexibility Act of 2013.

[29] The small-cap stocks in particular.

[30] This means of a "voluntary" nature. Leibowitz did not elaborate in a subsequent follow-up during the editing of this chapter.

There is a gentleman on the floor of the exchange, Jim McGuire, who we call Mr. Nickel because he is always proposing nickels.[31] He will be very happy that I brought this up. If, for example, we ran a market with a nickel increment, all the other markets would trade inside of us; consequently nickel pricing would have to be marketwide and enforced. I think it would be better for everyone involved if we had fewer little trades inside these spreads that are not really the effective spread.

A lot of people talk about volatility today. What they are really seeing is that the spread in the market is not the actual spread.[32] They are seeing a lot of activity around the actual spread in the stock that looks like volatility. What you are seeing, in fact, are tiny little trades constantly flickering in and out that actually do not reflect a stock's real price. That is very confusing to traders and investors.

I also believe that when people castigate high-frequency trading and blame high-frequency traders for manipulating share prices, it's not really high-frequency trading that they are talking about. What you are seeing are stocks that really should be trading in spreads of four cents. In other words, when somebody shows a bid, somebody else naturally sits on top of them. Now that is not a high-frequency trade.

My recommendation would be to start with wider pricing increments on some segment of the market. Unfortunately, we don't have a Petri dish to test this. It is hard to go into the lab and figure out how this will work. It is tough to have pilot projects with a couple of companies and to ask the issuer, "How would you like to be the poster child?" They will no doubt respond, "Well, maybe let someone else go first." At the end of the day, it has become really frustrating seeing how these stocks trade. We need to solve this. We also need to take action on a comprehensive review of equities market structure to regain confidence and to ensure a better capital marketplace in the future.

[31] "Many of the 3,000 floor workers call him the Chief, in deference to his status as one of the exchange's elder statesmen. The wiseguys on the floor call him Mr. Nickel and drop off small coins along with their order slips, because of his campaign to price stocks in units greater than a penny." See, Family atmosphere fades from NYSE's floor http://www.nytimes.com/2005/05/19/business/worldbusiness/19iht-floor.html?_r=0.
Source: *New York Times*, May 20, 2007.

[32] "Volatility usually increases during periods of rapid market decline or advancement. At these times, the bid-ask spread is much wider because market makers want to take advantage of—and profit from—the change. When securities are increasing in value, investors are willing to pay more, giving market makers the opportunity to charge higher premiums. When volatility is low and uncertainty and risk are at a minimum, the bid-ask spread is narrow."
Source: Investopedia.com.

Thank you everyone.

ROBERT SCHWARTZ: One more thing to do. It is a really sweet and wonderful thing. We thank our sponsors, because without your backing and support we couldn't be running this conference. We have had really outstanding speakers today. Thanks to all the panelists, our moderators, and I thank you Larry. I am very grateful that you came here today. And I have always felt that you, the people here in the audience, are another panel in your very special way. You are a big part of the success of this conference. You are a distinguished audience, in part because you are from industry, in part because of my academic colleagues who are here today, and also because the people from my classes, my Baruch students are here. I thank you all. (Applause)

There is one other person who I want to thank, Gretchen Schnee. Gretchen, come over here (Applause). Believe me, my thanks are heartfelt. Many of you have been to previous conferences so you will know that Toni Colaninno has worked tirelessly on them. Toni has relocated to Germany. Gretchen, who has stepped in to assume Toni's role, and has been absolutely superb. (Applause).

Now, everybody, let's get some real liquidity!

CPSIA information can be obtained
at www.ICGtesting.com
Printed in the USA
LVHW06*1151030618
579412LV00001B/10/P

9 783319 103495